J·E·W·I·S·H
ALTERNATIVES
IN
LOVE, DATING & MARRIAGE
PINCHAS STOLPER

NCSY/Orthodox Union/University Press of America

Co-published by:

National Conference of Synagogue Youth / Union
of Orthodox Jewish Congregations of America,
45 West 36th Street, New York, NY 10018
and
University Press of America, Inc., 4720 Boston Way, Lanham, MD 20706

ISBN (Cloth): 0-8191-4475-4
ISBN (Perfect): 0-8191-4476-2

Distributed in Israel by Mesorah Mafitzim/J. Grossman,
Rechov Bayit Vegan 90/5, Jerusalem

Produced by Olivestone Publishing Services

PRINTED IN THE UNITED STATES OF AMERICA

Contents

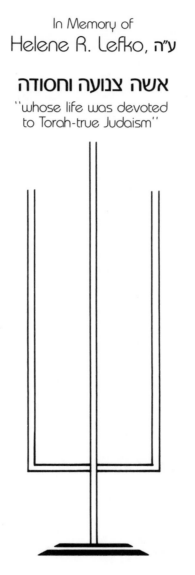

Published through the courtesy of the
HENRY, BERTHA and EDWARD ROTHMAN
FOUNDATION
Rochester, N.Y. • Circleville, Ohio • Cleveland

Foreword

by

Rabbi Aryeh Kaplan

After making an exhaustive study of human sexuality, a prominent anthropologist concluded, "Sex among humans is much closer to what your mother told you when you were a child. It's powerful and dangerous, offering great rewards and also great pain". In an era when sexual relationships are still often taken casually, his words deserve careful consideration.

Judaism has always taught that sex is "powerful and dangerous"; not to be taken casually. For one thing, sex brings the next generation into existence, and therefore, since the potential number of offspring of every liaison increases geometrically with every generation, every sexual act between two human beings has ramifications that can affect untold millions of human beings.

Beyond that, the Torah realizes that sex can totally change a person's psychology. Innumerable cases are cited where people are totally rational—in everything other than their sexual lives. Successful businessmen, who otherwise plan every facet of their lives with extreme care, are thus often willing to throw away everything for the sake of fleeting sexual pleasure.

Judaism does not see sex as something dirty or animal. Rather, the Torah sees sex as one of the most holy human endeavors. Indeed, the Torah's strictures surrounding sex can be compared to those surrounding the permissible uses of a Torah scroll. It is precisely because a Torah scroll is so sacred that the uses to which it can be put are so severely restricted. The same is true of sex.

A hint of this is found in the account of man's creation, where the Torah states, "God created the human in His image—in the image of God He created him—male and female He created him" (Genesis 1:27). The verse unambiguously states that the image of God is formed by man and woman together. This concept is echoed in numerous places in the Talmud and Midrash.

It is significant that in the Hebrew language there is no neuter; everything is either masculine or feminine. In conceptual terms, the masculine is seen as the power to give, while the feminine is the power to receive (This is true primarily in the abstract; it is recognized that in the real world, men and women both have masculine and feminine sides.)

In His role as Creator, God is seen as giving the world existence, and is hence portrayed as masculine. But in His role as accepting prayer, God is seen as feminine. Obviously, God Himself is above all gender. But when we speak of various aspects of our understanding of God, we use adjectives and descriptions, and one of them is gender. Thus, although the creative and providential aspects of God are seen as masculine, there is also a feminine aspect of the Divine, usually referred to as the *Shekhinah*.

When a male prophet sees a vision of the masculine aspect of the Divine, he sees it as having his own face. On the other hand, when he sees a vision of the female aspect of the Divine, he sees it as having the face of his wife. In the case of a prophetess, the role is reversed; she sees the feminine aspect as herself, and the masculine aspect as her husband. The reasons for this are beyond the scope of our present discussion, but on the simplest level, represent the fact that every prophet sees a vision through the spark of Divine in himself.

When a man and woman come together, they form the complete image of the Divine. This is a situation more wrought with holiness even than a Torah scroll. It is not without reason that the covenant of Abraham, which is the indelible mark of the Jew, involves the sexual organ.

There has long been a need for a book that presents the Jewish view that sex is both holy and beautiful, and, at the same time, dangerous if misused. My good friend, Rabbi Pinchas Stolper, has done an admirable job in producing such a book. It is a work that will go a long way in helping the contemporary community deal with the sexual revolution and the problems it has engendered.

Preface

Perhaps the most difficult challenge for a young American Jew is to adhere, in private and public life, to the traditional Torah regulations of male-female relationships while at the same time living and breathing the air of an American culture in which the rules have been relaxed, the barriers let down, and where permissiveness in sexual behavior has been accepted and approved by society-at-large as the norm. Where religious law demands restraint, and approves of sexual activity only within the carefully defined boundaries of marriage and private life, a young, intelligent American Jew, aware of the basic conflict between what religion teaches and society allows, yet no more immune to the influence of environment than any of his less aware American counterparts, struggles hard to reconcile the conflict, to choose a path of behavior and to resist temptation along the way.

That, however, so many *do succeed* in meeting the challenge of a more exacting standard of moral behavior, might suggest evidence of a natural inclination or inherent personal need for more clearly defined standards of wholesomeness, direction and purpose in life. That so many young people have changed previous modes of behavior and have adopted new ways of life based on traditional standards, despite the influence of America's media-produced sexual revolution, could attest to the existence of a basic human need for framework or structure in life and for the deeper satisfactions of spiritual experience and expression. One almost suspects it could be *permissiveness itself*, or, if not, then at least *permissiveness to excess*, that has challenged young people to question, and that has brought so many young Jewish people back to the threshold of Torah for acceptable and convincing answers.

But how can greater numbers of young people be expected to respond to the challenge of the Torah's ideology and practice, when, for the most part, we have failed to communicate the Torah's teaching in this area of life? Even though sex and all that surrounds it is no longer a hush topic in today's open society, the basic attitudes, standards and laws of Torah with regard to sex still remain the privileged possession of the few, unavailable to the public-at-large. Furthermore, how can the many young people who assimilate and intermarry, or who fall prey to the lure of the cult mystique, be called to account when we have failed to adequately take seriously the natural need of every human being for spiritual fulfillment and the expressed desire of so many contemporary Jews for initiation into the more substantial and authentic modes of religious observance, where either compromised or diluted forms of religious experience have failed to satisfy.

This is the hour to "act for the Lord". One must "know how to respond" to the challenge of secular modernity and to compete for the respect, allegiance and dedication of the best minds of contemporary American Jewish youth.

Thousands of searching, young Jews are still condemned to a life of assimilation, alienation, or intermarriage, largely because we are not doing enough to reach out to them. Even when they knock at our door we have not yet learned to respond adequately to their yearning for a life of spirituality. It is of little value to self-righteously condemn the community of secular or religiously compromising Jews for their inadequacies or failures. It is increasingly clear that all ideologies and approaches to Jewishness, with the singular exception of the uncompromised Torah way of life, have lost their attractiveness to Jewish youth, and that young people especially, are generally repelled by or simply disinterested in secular or non-Orthodox brands of compromised or watered down Jewishness.

There is no excuse when the Torah community takes lightly its responsibility to reach out—and to produce a literature which will reveal the inner light of Jewish thought in contemporary idiom.

Pinchas Stolper
New York, June 1984

Introduction

Jewish Alternatives in Love, Dating and Marriage is an attempt to suggest a variety of approaches for setting forth an authentic Jewish position on sex, family, and male-female relationships... the understanding of which is so crucial in preparation for successful marriage and responsible adulthood. The book is based largely on insights and approaches developed in discussions with young people from every background and in nearly every city of the United States during formal and informal meetings held under the auspices of NCSY, the National Conference of Synagogue Youth, during the eighteen years the author served as its National Director. The material of this book focuses, however, on those specific areas that concern young people of the "dating age" and does not, therefore, claim to cover all other related topics either in detail or in depth.

Discussions that concern the topic of sex, in keeping with the concept of sexual modesty, are best held with small homogeneous groups of young men, or young women, separately, and study or discussion sessions are best led by men or women whose religious devotion and sense of tact are taken for granted, who could approach the topic with attitudes that would encourage openness and sincere interest. Because give-and-take discussion sessions are almost always most valuable when they promote the interests of understanding and knowledge, it is best to avoid guilt and embarrassment.

Jewish Alternatives in Love, Dating and Marriage does not set forth the position or expectation of Halacha, Jewish law, with regard to any specific situation and is therefore not to be regarded as a "code of behavior" that would *instruct* an individual on how to respond or react in a *specific* circumstance. Instead, it suggests methods for dealing with a series of topics whose general category is *tsnius*, the Jewish concept and approach to matters of sex, family and moral conduct.

For guidance *concerning* specific problems or for answers to *particular* questions, an individual is advised to approach his own rabbi. Explanations or rulings that pertain to personal circumstance can best be rendered from the enlightened perspective of an open, honest and ongoing relationship between the rabbi and the individual concerned.

This book does not delve into the regulations and laws of "family purity" that pertain to marriage, such as *nidah, tevilah, mikveh*, etc. For an excellent, modern exposition of the laws of Family Purity, the reader is urged to consult Rabbi Norman Lamm's *Hedge of Roses*, (Feldheim Publishers) and for a unique and thorough study of the concept and practice of *mikveh*, the author recommends *Waters of Eden*, by Rabbi Aryeh Kaplan, published by NCSY.

The author makes little claim to originality. While some of the insights are his, others were adapted from classical and contemporary sources. Many are the outgrowth of the reactions of American Jewish young people themselves. *Mikol melamdai hiskalti, mitalmidai yoser mikulom*. "I have acquired wisdom from my teachers, but more so from my pupils".

Jewish Alternatives in Love, Dating and Marriage, originally published under the title "The Road to Responsible Jewish Adulthood", has been completely revised, rewritten and enlarged with the addition of a number of new chapters that reflect sensitivity to the ever-changing environment of America and to the many welcome recommendations of students and friends.

The first edition, published in 1967, was read by a number of individuals who offered critical comments, to whom I extend my sincere appreciation. I am especially grateful to Rabbi Norman Lamm for his many suggestions, to Rabbi and Mrs. Jack Steinhorn, the late Rabbi Israel Klavan, Yaakov Kornreich and Meyer Krentzman. The first edition was read in mimeographed form by more than two dozen young people. Their observations were of great value in determining the book's final form. Their frankness and friendship is deeply appreciated.

This edition has been read by Dr. Joseph Kaminetsky, Yaakov Kornreich, Marla Corush, Dr. Reuven Bulka, and Rabbi Shmuel Himmelstein to whom I offer my gratitude. Their critical comments are appreciated. My special thanks to Dr. Judith B. Katz for her special efforts in reviewing and rewriting sections of the manuscript, and to David Olivestone whose good taste has made possible the attractive appearance of this volume.

I recall with gratitude the inspiration and devotion to Jewish tradition of my father, Rabbi David Bernard Stolper, zts''l, and my mother Mrs. Nettie Stolper.

I dedicate this volume to my wife Elaine who personifies the nobility and goodness of the Jewish wife and mother. May we be worthy to enjoy the continued growth in Torah and *yiras shamayim* of our children and grandchildren.

"For the Lord your God walks in the midst of your community to protect you . . . therefore your community must be holy, that He may not see anything indecent, unseemly, and turn away from you".

TWO NOTES

There are sections of the book in which the author speaks primarily to young men, or to young women, and in these sections he will, naturally, address himself accordingly. In other cases, however, and especially in today's era of confused sex roles where most messages apply to both male and female, for the sake of practicality and easy flow, the author employs a general or collective term, instead of the more awkward and cumbersome 'boy-girl' or 'man-woman' combination where such phraseology might disturb the rhythm, ease, or fluidity of style.

The term "*tsnius*", is a Hebrew term that embraces the various notions of modesty, humility, decency, privacy and self-restraint—qualities of behavior and character that govern the manner in which a person should relate to his fellow man—attitudes with which to approach, fulfill and perform our responsibilities and obligations to Almighty God.

To "walk *humbly* with God" also carries the meaning of hiddenness, inwardness and privacy.

J·E·W·I·S·H
ALTERNATIVES
IN
LOVE, DATING & MARRIAGE

Ben Zoma said:
Who is strong?
He who subdues his passions.
Avot 4:1

1
Searching for
Authentic Goals

In America everyone minds everyone else's business. Sex, love and marriage are the major topics of newspapers, television, literature, the movies and the stage. Sex is America's major obsession, and one of its most lucrative industries. Pornography in its various manifestations is a billion dollar business.

For a Jew, though, sex is nobody else's business, nobody's but his own. In Judaism, marital relations require absolute privacy, and it is this privacy that has permitted Jewish marriages to remain holy and that encourages the deepening of interpersonal relationships. This Jewish abhorrence of allowing the public exposure of a private activity has nothing at all to do with guilt, but is rather an ingrained respect for privacy and recognition of the fact that the protection of privacy is a basic human need and requirement.

Deluged as we are by a torrent of written and graphic material in a society obsessed with sex, we often wonder: What is the Jewish point of view?

The hallmark of the Jewish attitude toward sex is privacy, modesty and holiness. Whatever happens between two people does not belong in tomorrow's headlines. And it is mostly for this reason that Jews have been reluctant to publish books and articles in English for the general public which discuss in public that which we believe should be discussed only in private.

THE CREATIVE LIFE FORCE OF A PEOPLE

The happy hookers, the sensuous psychiatrists and the playboy philosophers haven't much in common, but they are united in proclaiming the advent of a "new age of freedom" between the sexes.

But people who are sensitive and thoughtful will not allow themselves to be taken in. A counterreaction has begun, and with it a search for values and standards which recognize that a human is a spiritual being, capable of reaching beyond his or her body and of responding to the urgings of the soul, a being who takes God into account and who searches for a link with eternity when making life's major decisions.

Many people have begun to ask: Is sex a mere biological impulse or is it the life force and creative impulse of a People? Is it simply a private matter between two "consenting adults" or does it govern the quality of life? Isn't life devalued and deformed when sex is declared open and "free" and, consequently, isn't such an attitude destructive of the social fabric and the very essence of human society?

When we think of sex, do we think only of copulation? Or do we realize that sexual energy influences so much of our human personality—connecting each individual to family, community and people and through these to the past and future of mankind? Do we realize too, that the human environment, the very landscape of life and civilization is a precarious achievement that depends to a very great extent on our attitudes toward sexual and interpersonal relationships? Or that many societies have actually collapsed because the family and morality collapsed first—because people became interested only in the pursuit of selfish, ego-satisfying pleasure, and lost sight of anyone else: their partner, the unborn, their family or the values of the Godly Kingdom beyond man.

I invite the reader to consider his or her personal stake in finding the right answers. Though our momentary impulses may sometimes lead us astray, logic, our values and our fear of consequences should motivate us to strengthen the only code of interpersonal relationships which has the potential for bringing us into harmony with both God and society. To the

Jew, sex can never be a matter of fun and games. It is one of the few matters of truly life and death importance to every individual, to society and the continuity of the Jewish people.

IS THERE AN OBJECTIVE RIGHT WAY?

The purpose of this book is to help young people discover that they still have a choice between the "new freedom" (which is nothing but old-fashioned immorality) so urgently promoted by the media and a standard of conduct which has stood the test of thousands of years, and offers the only proven, reliable avenue to the achievement of human happiness and fulfillment. In this book, I hope to point out the likely consequences of these choices. I will try to describe *The Jewish Alternative*, a way of life that has proven itself to generations of people, as a potential source and sturdy foundation for the realization of successful living and self-fulfillment. In my opinion, the "new" standard of acceptable social conduct between the sexes is a path fraught with danger, which does not work. It has been foisted upon us, in large measure, by certain commercial and often criminal interests which have turned pornography and the "philosophy" which underlies it into big business, making sexual liberation ring on the cash registers of a contrived revolution. Unfortunately many honest and well-meaning people have been taken in and deceived by this propaganda or by some aspects of it.

The downhill plunge of American moral standards continues apace. Each year new pornographic magazines and movies find the "courage" to go farther than their predecessors. Sexual conduct is now governed by the "consenting adult" principle and sexual aberrations are now called "alternative lifestyles". The institutions of family and marriage are under constant attack. The idea of premarital chastity is becoming a relic to many young people. We are told that there is no objective "right way", that each individual has the right to exercise the option of discovering what rules are best for him or herself.

My advice to today's young people is that before they accept any of the above attitudes, they owe it to themselves to do some in-depth investigating.

Is there an objective "right way" that has stood the test of time?

Is there a "proven standard" that meets the physical, psychological and spiritual needs of people?

Is there truth to the claim equating permissiveness with happiness?

Is this modern "new morality" an original concept, or has civilization already tried similar approaches, and with what results or consequences?

Does Jewish morality offer a unique alternative, not to be found in other approaches?

Is sex too often a transaction wherein a young woman pays with her body for dates, popularity, friendship, going steady, or a false sense of security? If so, is she selling herself too cheaply?

Does sexual freedom promote greater social and emotional health?

A Cornell study, which involved observation of the population of an entire section of Nova Scotia for ten years by a team of psychologists and psychiatrists found "the highest prevalence of psychoneurotic symptoms among the group with the least sexual restraint".

Dr. Dana L. Farmsworth, Director of the Harvard University Health Services writes that "The experiences in our college and other psychiatric services lead us to believe that those who ignore conventional standards are surely no more effective or happy than those who observe them. In fact…nonconformists (experience) more depression, anxiety, agitation, loss of self-esteem and other inhibiting emotional conflict than those who manage to adhere to their ideals".

Objective scientific evidence supports the following conclusions: (a) Young people with premarital sexual experience are more likely to exhibit neurotic patterns and suffer from impaired mental health than those without such experience; (b) Premarital sex does not promote better sexual adjustment in marriage; (c) The most successful marriages are between two people, neither of whom has experimented before marriage with sexual activity.

Documented studies by sociologist Robert O. Blood, Jr. also reveal that "premarital intercourse is associated more closely with broken relationships than with strengthened ones; (that) twice as many engagements are broken among couples who had intercourse than among those who did not;…(that) both divorce and adultery are more common among those couples who indulge in premarital intercourse".

If the above conclusions are true, then where can one find a way of life which fosters and promotes a healthy, constructive and positive relationship between the sexes? And if the traditional Jewish point of view offers a meaningful and viable alternative, how can a person learn more about it?

In the pages that follow, the author will raise questions and suggest answers that he hopes will stimulate his readers to search, think, study, and investigate in the hope that they will develop a deeper understanding of the Jewish religious outlook. It is his hope, too, that it will lead to a fuller appreciation of the Torah view—and its full observance as well.

2
Love and Family

THE SOURCE OF MORAL LAW

God, who created man, knows what is best for him and supervises the destiny of His own creation. Man and the moral law which, according to Jewish thought, must govern man's life, have one origin, one source, one Creator. The notion that religion and life are two separate entities is foreign to Jewish thought. The idea that an unbridgeable gap separates everyday law from religious morality is not a Jewish idea. That the secular and the holy are two separate worlds is one of the non-Jewish notions partially responsible for the social crisis that threatens the stability of contemporary life. To the classical Jewish way of thinking, all law—civil, religious, or moral—flows from a common source. The same God who created man and woman commanded a single set of laws, called Torah, to govern with equal force and authority in all areas of human activity, without exception. It would stand to reason, therefore, that the God who created man, with a set of needs, energies, abilities, and ambitions, would also teach him how best to meet, expend, utilize, and realize them. Torah, which perceives the human being as a miniature sanctuary and views all human activity as potentially sacred, contains this teaching and offers the ideal guide for human and social living and fulfillment.

Surrounded as we are by a frightening breakdown in family, social and interpersonal relationships and by a spreading crisis of sexual identity, it is essential that we become conscious of the fact that just as God created the

7

universe, with all the physical laws which govern it, so too did He create mankind and the laws which govern every facet of human life and endeavor. To ignore these laws is not only to defy God, but to forfeit our opportunity for a mature, creative and meaningful existence.

FROM LOVE OF MAN TO LOVE OF GOD

Who is God? He is the creator of the cosmos, creator of mountains and seas, animals and birds, man and woman. He is also the creator of love and compassion, generosity and tenderness, justice and mercy, sensitivity and holiness.

The Almighty wants us to emulate and imitate Him, to follow his example, to fulfill and perfect ourselves by aspiring to higher levels of spirituality and holiness.* We can *best* imitate God and express our love of Him by learning to love man, God's own remarkable and greatest creation.

Where does human love most easily, most naturally, and most frequently develop? It is in the various dynamic relationships that bind husband and wife, and later, parent and child. These relationships reflect the expressions of caring and concern, solicitude and sacrifice, affection, regard, kindness, devotion, warmth and sharing that we classify under the umbrella definition of love, as the term 'love' is understood by man. In order to better love God, therefore, it is well first to have experienced the love of man; that is, to have loved, been loved, and to have understood and experienced all the emotions, aspects, and expressive avenues of the loving relationship.

If a person can deeply appreciate and respect those to whom he is most closely related, he may finally discover the possibility of love for his friend, or fellow man, as himself. The commandment of the Torah to "love your fellow as yourself" can also be understood to mean "love your fellow because he is like yourself", which means that just as *you* were created in God's image, so was *he*; that just as *you* have needs and feelings, so too has *he*.

Once a person has achieved this understanding and practice of love for people in the physical world, he more easily can intensify his love for God who is more abstract and distant.

The process of learning to love God and of establishing a personal rela-

---

*"Just as He is merciful, so too shall you be merciful..." (Talmud Shabbos 133B).

tionship with God should begin and grow out of the experiences and habits of early childhood. As we begin to love and appreciate our parents, we develop a sense of gratitude for all the favors they bestow, which we should soon recognize as pleasures and blessings that have their source in God.

Another way to learn the love of God is by emulating our parents' and teachers' love of God, by respecting the values by which our parents and teachers live. This is especially so when they conscientiously observe the Heaven-given Commandments, the *mitzvos*, which, after all, are the only way we are able to relate to God—*in deed*. The *mitzvos*, we soon realize, are the only tools we have for perfecting ourselves, for taming the animal and elevating the more primitive in ourselves, and for reaching toward God.

THE UNIQUE ROLE OF THE FAMILY

In this book, our concern is with personal and interpersonal relationships, and the effect of each person's behavior on the uniqueness, value, sanctity and dignity of each other individual.

Our Rabbis ask: "Why was each individual born uniquely different"? They answer: "So that he should be able to say to himself 'For *my* sake was the world created'". If our concern is for the individual, why should this book begin with a discussion of the family? Simply put, it is because the family structure is the one human social institution that is most indispensable for creating and forming the individual. Without the family, there can be no individual, not only biologically—but in no other sense either.

Two people must act in unison in order to create a third. The highest act of human creativity calls for two to act as *one* in order to bring forth a new individual. If two can act as *one*, they can draw a new soul down to earth and create a new human being, making God a third partner in a new miracle of Creation. God has given man the ability to duplicate His own greatest feat of Creation by creating a child. When we create a child we literally *play God*. But if the child is the product of lust, or physical passion alone, if he or she is created through the rejection of God's law—then what kind of child have we created?

But the drama of man's partnership with God in the drama of creation does not end with the birth of a child. After birth, too, the father and mother must live together if a family is to be created in which the children can be reared and educated to develop into men or women capable of fulfilling their own human and spiritual destiny. Each person is, to a large extent, what his or her parents make him or her and if the parents are successful their children may even be better than they. Jewish parents have always hoped that they will succeed in rearing children who will be better than themselves, who will be more capable of fulfilling their own individual human and spiritual destinies. This explains why parents are not usually jealous of the accomplishments of their children. Thus we find in the Talmud (Sanhedrin 105B), "a person is jealous of everyone else, except for his son and pupil".

In the historic Jewish view, it is the family and not the synagogue that is considered *the* basic institution of Jewish life and society. In fact, most of the crucial acts and experiences of Jewish living call for a family setting. The synagogue at best plays a secondary role.

The Jewish family has long been a model of harmony, love, and stability; the envy of the entire civilized world. The social evils that tend to disrupt and destroy modern society, such as divorce, prostitution, adultery, wife-beating, and juvenile delinquency, were until recent times almost unknown among traditional, unassimilated Jews. While observant Jews in America have also been affected by this generation's tendency to solve marital problems through divorce, there is a qualitative difference of considerable weight between observant Jews and other groups.

Marriage is not optional for a Jewish man, but is obligatory. The Talmud (Shabbos 31A) states that in the world to come, the first three questions asked of a man will be: "Did you buy and sell in good faith? Did you have a set time for Torah study? Did you raise a family?" The single life is regarded as a misfortune, and a good wife the chief delight of a man's existence. It was and is easy to obtain a Jewish divorce, but relatively few have done so. Jews who observe tradition, as set forth by Jewish law, take family life very seriously and create stable, strong and supportive family environments. They work hard at their marriages and resort to divorce only after many and extensive attempts to keep a marriage together have definitely failed.

Every Jewish man is expected to marry in order to fulfill the commandment of having children and raising a family. "Be fruitful and multiply" is a basic *mitzvah*. The family bond and its relationships are sanctified. Marriage and family are integral parts of the Divine plan. The love which attracts man and woman to each other is sacred in the eyes of God. Jews see the family as the essential force in the development of a God-fearing individual, and the creation of a *home* in which God dwells. If this home is dedicated to God, and *His* word reigns supreme there, it becomes the fulcrum for the entire structure of Jewish life.

The purpose of the family includes not only the satisfaction of the basic human need for comradeship, love, reproduction and raising children, but the total development of the individual, and, on the larger scale, the development of all of mankind to its fullest potential.

According to Torah laws, sex is not permitted outside of marriage. Sex is not simply an "act" which brings *two bodies together*, but an integral part of marriage, bringing *two people together*, not for fun or satisfaction alone, but in order to make it possible for two people to become truly one. In Judaism, sex is holy because it implies much more than the uniting of two bodies for a few moments of pleasure, but for always. Marriage means much more than two people who share a bedroom. It means two people who share a home and enjoy a relationship *so* successfully that in thinking and acting as one they are prepared to share their life and unite for the bringing of children into the world. The sex act is so significant and powerful that it is not only the point of origin of all of mankind, it enables a couple to bring a soul from its heavenly abode down to earth, where it can assume the shape and form of a new human being.

If the relationship between two people is based on sex or pleasure alone, it implies that the moment either partner finds someone else who promises "better sex", they will leave each other and take new partners. However, if a relationship is based on love and made permanent through marriage, and if the family is a holy unit, then two partners have made a lasting commitment, each to the other, to help, support, and encourage each other in sickness, tragedy, poverty, hardship, and even death.

The relationship of man and woman is unique because only the human being is created in the "image" or reflection of God. Possibly by achieving a deeper insight into the uniqueness of the human being, we might better appreciate the unique opportunity we have to create a special relationship with the opposite sex, of uniting two into one, which has the potential of achieving overtones of the unique qualities of God himself.

THE HUMAN AND THE ANIMAL: BASIC DIFFERENCES

Why is a human child so helpless and dependent at birth; why is the difference between human and most animal newborns so pronounced and radical? Some of the contrast between the spiritual potential of human and animal can be understood by analyzing the total helplessness of the human infant.

Without a mother's constant attention, the human infant is completely lost. The infant is totally dependent for physical, psychological and emotional well-being upon the care and life support system of its mother. In fact, studies reveal that even if feeding is maintained, but emotional contacts like hugging, kissing, and talking are withdrawn, the child may deteriorate and eventually die. The human infant appears to be all "potential", raw material as it were, awaiting the attention and care of its parents, attention comprised of the love, guidance, protection, and support that makes growth, maturation, learning and development possible.

In the animal world, however, observation reveals quite the reverse. A fish, for example, functions as a fully independent individual from the moment it is hatched. Immediately from birth, the fish is capable of swimming, breathing, and feeding itself. Some fish may never even see their parents. The simplicity of biological design and function obviates the need for parental support. There are no skills to teach, no emotions to convey, no knowledge to pass on. There is no civilization, history or tradition, no need for teaching fish to become links in a continuing chain. Each generation of fish is an exact replica of the generation from which it derived.

The salmon, for instance, offers an excellent and easily observable example. Soon after a mature female salmon swims upstream to deposit her eggs, she turns back downstream to the sea and dies. The male salmon, drawn by instinct, deposits his sperm on the eggs already laid, then follows the same current back downstream and disappears into oblivion. Before long, tiny salmon hatch from the deposit of eggs and sperm on the banks of the stream, and begin downstream toward entry into the ocean where they will grow, live, and develop. As they mature, they too will swim upsteam to repeat the pattern of their unknown parents. The infant salmon knows nothing of either parent. Why should he?

The more complex the form of life, however, the more necessary, lasting, and intense is the relationship that develops between parent and child. In the animal kingdom on a scale from simple to complex, one notes the parent-child relationship also moving from simple to complex, in both duration of time and development of family-type associations.

Because fish have nothing to teach their young, no tradition to give over, no skills or language to impart, there is no need to train their off-spring. There is no need for family—there are no traditions, relationships, discipline, goals, or ideals.

The human infant is *so helpless* because it has *so much* to learn: traditions, relationships, ideals, and goals. For this reason, the performance of a mother or father in teaching, inspiring, or motivating will actually largely determine the kind of person the infant will become, the degree of progress and influence and the flow of continuity, from one era to another, of human civilization. The very survival of the ideals of the past depends upon the ability of parents and teachers to transmit, inspire, motivate and mold. Parents teach children to use the knowledge already gained by men and women of past generations for the improvement of their own present and future lives, for the benefit and general welfare of society at large, and for the intelligent responses required by the challenges of new situations and times.

The relationship to parents must be so strong that the child feels that he or she is the bearer of human destiny: each child must grow up believing that all that mankind has achieved since the beginning of time—and must accomplish until the end of time—is in his or her hands. Each person is a link in the chain of civilization, the bearer of human destiny and purpose, and if one link breaks, the chain may snap.

If young men and women would only consider what will become of them if they ignore their spiritual-human potential, and allow the animal in them free reign, they may be more careful not to behave like "animals" in interpersonal relationships. If they consider that the sexual attraction which draws them to each other is also a powerful spiritual force, they will take special care not to allow their physical drives to control their spiritual drives—and will not allow the instinct of the moment to pervert or even destroy the potential of eternity.

Consider the crucial nature of speech in the hypothetical model of a man-woman relationship illustrated below: A young man and woman are locked in a room from which there is no escape. There are no doors, windows, books, television or radio sets. Both are provided with ample food, drink, and a sofa, yet are scantily clad. But neither can speak. Thus with no knowledge of how they have arrived or of how they may escape, they may soon find themselves involved in the only activities available: eating, drinking, and engaging in a sexual relationship. Suddenly, however, if the ability to speak is restored, with the resulting discovery that one is Danish and the other Greek, their relationship may well come to a very abrupt end. Radical differences in tastes, languages, thoughts, politics, ideals, likes and dislikes would leave them with no basis for communication or no common ground at all. They will probably find it impossible to understand or appreciate each other. Quarreling will easily follow; end of relationship.

The Torah (Unkelus) describes man as a "speaking being", and therein lies another distinction between man and animal. Speech is the human characteristic that enables men to communicate, to develop their physical and spiritual potential, to exercise their choices, to establish values, to act in history, to perpetuate tradition, and to live purposeful lives. Speech is the verbal articulation of thought and should guide men and women in living *responsible lives*. And since the human being is set apart and distinguished from the animal by the unique gift of speech that is his alone, it is speech which *alone* can express and convey the ideals and goals of a human society that must be used *responsibly* in the creation of meaningful and dignified interpersonal relationships. Since humans are essentially speaking beings, speech must take precedence in the creation of responsible interpersonal relationships.

Unlike God, who is unique and alone, the human being reaches his or her truest potential, and expresses his or her God-like qualities best, when he or she lives with a partner. To become a fulfilled human being, "it is not good that man live alone", man must find a partner, a mate, a helper, in order to achieve the *good* as defined by the Torah.

WHY WAS WOMAN CREATED?

Almost immediately after the creation of the first man, the Lord remarked: "This is not good, for man to be alone. I shall make him a helpmate, for (literally: opposite or against) him". (Genesis 2:18). Rabbi Samson Raphael Hirsch observes that the Torah phrase did not read: "It is not good for man to be alone", but "This is not good; man being alone", implying rather that when a person is alone, good cannot exist. The completion of the state of good in creation was not man, but woman. As the Talmud elaborates, "only through his wife does man *become a man*".

When it describes the creation of woman, the Torah teaches that since woman was created from the rib of man, from another human, she represents a higher level in creation than man, who was created from earth. When we examine creation as depicted in the Bible, we see that God created the world in progressive stages; from lower to higher; from simpler to more complex; from the chaos, confusion, and material of Day One, to the order, perfection, and spiritual qualities of Day Seven, the Sabbath. From the first day, when darkness covered the earth, to the sixth day when God created man and woman.

Creation reaches its heights on the seventh day, the day of Sabbath rest, which is the day of messianic perfection when man emerges as a spiritual being who has overcome his dependence on materialism and the tyranny of *things*. First God created space, time, energy, and the matter of inanimate elements and compounds; later He created plants and trees; then insects, fish and birds; still later animals; and *finally* man, on the sixth day.

Since woman was created after man, between his creation and the coming of the Sabbath, woman represents the highest stage of creation. In fact, when woman was created, the Torah for the first time declared that creation was *very* good. What was missing when man was created, the one last element still necessary before mankind could be established in the Garden of Eden and before the Sabbath could arrive? Woman.

A specific description of the biological function of women is explicitly stated in the Biblical narrative of creation: "And Adam called his wife's name Eve for she would be the *mother* of all life". (Genesis, 3:20). Marriage and family, integral to the Divine plan for the creation of mankind, are not arbitrary or artificial institutions "foisted" upon the human stituation, but rather lie at the very essence of human nature. "Therefore shall man leave his father and his mother and cleave unto his wife and they shall be one flesh" (Genesis, 2:24) follows immediately upon creation of Eve. The Ra'avad interprets the passage beautifully:

> It is for this reason that God saw fit to change the order of creation when He came to man. For had He created both man and woman from the earth, independent of each other, each one would go his or her own way. Husband and wife would not be designated one for the other, to live together, for they would have been created separately. Instead, God created woman *from* man

so that they would live together as one unit in marriage, each one needing the other for completion of themselves.

This does not imply that the Torah mandated specific roles for *all* women or *all* men, for to do so would be to lose touch with reality and the diversity of human nature. Life situations are much too complex for such simplistic attitudes. But this does not mean that certain roles are not viewed by the Torah as being natural roles for both men and women. So the fact that familial and marital responsibilities are the natural role for women is a concept that goes back to the Divine plan of creation, beginning with Eve and continuing through the entire Bible and Talmud.

WHAT IS JEWISH MARRIAGE?

Until recent years, most people took the institution of marriage for granted, never wondering at its almost universal acceptance. But in today's society, where no aspect of life escapes close and rational scrutiny, one must not hold back from investigating the institution of marriage as objectively as possible, in order to better understand and appreciate its significance for modern society.

Why are marriage and the family so basic to human society? Why should a *"single"*, *"happy"* man willingly surrender his freedom and independence to share his life with a complete *"stranger"*? Why should he want to feed this "stranger", house her, clothe her, support and educate *"her"* children? Why does a man assume these burdens, obligations and responsibilities? Voluntarily! And yet even in an era when marriage and the family are under attack, with young people daily exposed to propaganda promoting "alternative life styles", actual statistics indicate that as high a percentage of young people are marrying as ever before. The impulse to create a permanent family relationship is part of our very being, involving much more than a desire for sex, which is readily available outside of marriage. Perhaps we seek to love and to be loved; perhaps we need structure and self-respect, a home in which to grow and build, a family to mold and children to raise.

For these reasons, Jewish law strongly urges that people marry, and the earlier they marry, the better. In fact, in many observant families, it is common for young people's education to be completed *after* marriage, so that the young people can accomplish life's goals together, rather than waiting out a long period of tension and frustration before marriage.

Marriage is a mysterious force that calls man and woman to unite in a partnership to build a home in which God will feel welcome and dwell, a platform on which to inscribe the major points of life's program.

In addition, the Torah regards lifelong celibacy in men as sinful, a repudiation of a religious obligation and the blessings that follow from marriage. The Talmud (*Yevamos* 62B) clearly states that "he who spends his days without a wife, has no joy, no blessing, no good" in his life. But Torah law also contains a built-in bill of rights which gives the Jewish woman a unique status and position in the home, based on the Torah command that no matter how poor or troubled a man may be, with regard to his wife, "he may not diminish her support, her clothes or her conjugal rights". (Shemos 21: 10)

SEX IN MARRIAGE

Marital relations are, therefore, not merely a permissible factor in Jewish marriage, but an obligation called for by Torah law. For without man and woman joining together, on a regular basis, as *one flesh*, no marriage is complete. Sexual union within a marriage serves not only the purpose of creating children, but also promotes the overwhelming value intimacy has in strengthening the family bond as a single unit, spiritually and physically.

Unlike various Christian and non-Christian teachings, which insist that marital relations are only for the sake of procreation, Jewish law has always recognized that these intimate bonds play a broader and more comprehensive role in the relationship between two married people. Even when conception is not possible, as during pregnancy, for example, periodic marital relations are obligatory. Torah law singles out the Sabbath and Holidays as special occasions during which the marital *mitzvah* should be observed, as another way of celebrating, elevating and sanctifying these special days. Similarly, the Talmud directs that "It is a husband's duty to *intimately remember* his wife before he leaves on a trip". (*Yevamos* 62b)

The mystical Kabbalah teaches that "the *Shechinah*, or Divine Presence, only dwells in a home when a man is married and cohabits with his wife" (Zohar I 122A), for "marital relations are the highest expression of the intimate, deep, personal relationship that can exist between man and woman. On this level, marital relations are raised to holiness and purity". (*Moshe Meiselman*)

That sex is *much more* than just another marital *duty* is obvious from numerous statements in the Bible and Talmud. To quote one source, (Talmud *Eruvin*), "Rav Bruna said in the name of Rav, 'Whoever sleeps in a room in which dwell a man and his wife, of him the Torah says, *You have driven the wives of my people out of the home of her pleasures'*".

Sexual union helps to strengthen one of the most intimate bonds one person can possibly establish with another person. It is a primary, natural, and spiritual force which involves our total personalities at the deepest levels of our being. Sexual union is an intensely private, personal matter which, together with other personality factors, constitutes the cement which transforms two strangers into loving, intimate, lifelong companions, committed to each other and to the building of a Jewish family. But the Torah's laws of *tsnius* (modesty, humility, and privacy) create an environment of restraint, self-respect, and self-discipline that underlie the ban on sexual relations before marriage, so that sex will remain a potent force for the higher good of creating an exclusive and highly meaningful, permanent relationship after marriage. These laws insure that the physical impulse will be reserved for the chosen *one*, as an instrument of love, devotion, responsibility and personal fulfillment within marriage. The regulations of *tsnius* teach us to master and control our appetites, rather than be controlled by them. They also train us for that time when, once married, we will again be called upon to exercise self-discipline in the observance of the laws of *the Sanctity of the Family (taharas hamishpacha)*. These laws of family purity insure that for a given period each month, respect, affection, comradeship, and all the *other* impulses and factors that bind two people, *except* for the physical, be allowed to dominate the relationship of husband and wife.

While this is not the place for a detailed discussion of the laws of the Sanctity of the Family, we will outline some basic concepts here. Jewish law forbids sexual contact, or any physical expression of love between husband and wife, from the onset of her menstrual period until at least seven days after the end of the menstrual flow, for a total separation of twelve days or more, depending on the length of the individual woman's flow. At the end of this period, the wife immerses herself in a specially constructed and specially filled pool of water, known as *Mikveh*. It is only then that husband and wife may resume normal physical relations.

One of the most rewarding features of the Jewish laws of Family Sanctity is that they ensure a periodic renewal of the marriage relationship.

There is little need to explain that the yearning and pain of missing a loved one serves to bring about a fresh awareness of how deep the relationship really is. The love-sex relationship is nurtured as much through anticipation, longing, and expectation as through fulfillment. It is impossible to enjoy food without first growing hungry. A person who is constantly stuffed can hardly be expected to enjoy a delicious meal. While the analogy of sex to food can be taken too far, it does help us understand the role of boredom and satiety in anything that relates to physical pleasure. Each monthly period of waiting again recreates the eager and joyous anticipation of the marriage day. The marriage of a couple which observes the Torah's laws of Family Sanctity has the potential, when followed properly, of becoming a series of honeymoons, and should never become monotonous, habitual, or boring. Maybe this explains why religious Jewish marriages tend to be much happier and sturdier than most. Instead of rejecting love and sex, the Torah provides an opportunity for re-enacting, month after month, the drama of courtship, first without sexual contact then followed again by the loving union of husband and wife. It is this monthly reunion that makes possible deeper, more intensive relationships, which transform a physical act into a deeply personal, spiritual and emotional experience.

Only a Jew who observes the laws of Family Sanctity can understand how King Solomon's Biblical book, the Song of Songs, which describes two lovers, could be thought of by Rabbi Akiva as being "the holy of holies", a description of the loving relationship between God and the Jewish people. Only a religious Jew can understand how the yearning of two people for each other could have been employed in the Song of Songs to describe the mystical love and yearning of the Jewish people for its ultimate beloved, God, and God's love for the Jewish people.

While marriage demands an intimate, physical relationship, it is far more than sex. Only the Jew has been given a practical formula that succeeds in keeping sex basic to marriage, while at the same time restraining and preserving it so that intimacy does not become monotonous and unappealing. And yet at the same time, it allows other vital factors in marriage to develop in a healthy and constructive fashion.

The Jewish laws of Family Sanctity teach us that, to quote Norman Lamm, "Love does not grow stale in such an environment. A young woman's dreams remain fresh, her visions vital, her hopes radiant throughout life. All of life presents the opportunity of becoming a perpetual honeymoon. Her dreams are not defeated by success and frustrated by fulfillment". (For a unique and extensive explanation of the concept and *mitzvos* of the *Mikveh*, the reader is referred to a beautiful book by Aryeh Kaplan, of blessed memory, *Waters of Eden—The Mystery of the Mikveh*, published by the National Conference of Synagogue Youth.)

It is interesting to note that the world's highest divorce rate is to be found in American society, where sexual freedom and experimentation outside of marriage are not only permitted, but promoted. On the other hand, Jews, especially religious Jews who reject the idea of pre-marital "testing", but believe that good sex and mature love will come as the result of a good marriage, enjoy the lowest divorce rate and the most stable family life.

3
Means and Ends

The Torah does not accept the view that man's body and its physical functions are base, evil or shameful in any way. In Jewish tradition, sex is not sinful, nor is the body considered evil. Such notions are strictly non-Jewish in origin, and emanate primarily from pagan sources which found their way into Christianity, and from Christianity into the general Western culture. In an article entitled, "The Nuns that Quit", Jane O'Leary, a former nun says, "I wish that the sisters who taught me in elementary school and high school had given marriage its due. I grew up believing that virginity and perfection were synonymous". Sister Judith Tate of the Benedictines states, "In religious communities a negative celibacy has claimed first attention for centuries. The premise seemed to be that if a sister could eradicate her sexuality she could stand a better chance of being 'holy'". Sister Judith, in *Journal*, April 1967, explains that this concept arose from the attitude that "sexuality, especially feminine sexuality, was a necessary but obscene invention...It was fairly simple to establish shame about the fact of womanhood...In some cases it became part of a virtue to make oneself unattractive, for attractiveness was sexual lure. Hence mirrors were banished, heads were shaved, curves were flattened—all in the name of virtue".

The Torah takes a very different view by speaking of *man* and of all creation as "good". (Genesis, 1:31). The phenomenon of man and woman, with their many differences, is a wondrous manifestation of God's basic design, and sex is an instrument for the fulfillment of God's will. As with most instruments, it is potentially good if controlled and utilized for its intended purpose; dangerous if not. The record of the abuse and misuse of sex through prostitution, rape, pornography, crime, and even murder are examples of what results when something which carries the potential for so much good is misdirected or allowed to go out of control.

"Man" is directed to enjoy the world. In the Torah view, all human pleasures have been established for man's enjoyment, in order to motivate him to involve himself in the affairs of the world. But pleasure and enjoyment must be controlled by, and be subservient to, the laws, limitations, and conditions set by the Torah. The God who created us, who gave us our lives and fashioned our bodies, understands the limitations that will ensure lasting happiness, along with physical, mental and spiritual health and well-being. Sex is a positive good, a vital impulse, and a basic function that is essential to the survival and well-being of humanity. It is the key to human continuity and gives man the opportunity for extending life to eternity. With it, man and woman are partners with God in the work of creation. It becomes sinful only when misused, as when we model our personal behavior after the behavior of the animals who live by instinct rather than the dictates of the Torah; for the Torah teaches mankind to rise above the animal and employ thought, choice and self-control.

One of the most beautiful introductions to the Jewish attitude toward marital relations is contained in the *Igeres Hakodesh* (or Holy Letter), ascribed to the Ramban, Nachmanides, the great thinker of the Middle Ages:

> Marital relations are holy, pure and clean, when done in the correct manner, at the correct time, and with the correct attitude; and whoever says that there is something disgraceful and loathesome is gravely mistaken . . . All believers in the Torah believe that the Almighty created all according to His great wisdom and did not create anything which was intrinsically disgraceful. For, if we say that marital relations are intrinsically evil and disgraceful, then so are those parts of the human body, and if so, how did God create them? But God is pure of spirit and nothing comes from Him which is intrinsically evil and He created man and woman and created all of their organs. But the matter is

thus. For just as the hands of a human being can write a Torah and can create the highest sanctity, and at that time they are high and praiseworthy, and when they steal and murder they are evil and loathesome, so too in this area of life.

Without desire and impulse, mankind could not exist. The Medrash says of man's physical desires and drives: "Were it not for *that* impulse, a man would not build a house, marry a wife, beget children or conduct business affairs". (Genesis Raba IX, 7)

In describing the first human sexual encounter, the Torah employs the adjective *knowledge* to describe intercourse: "And Adam *knew* his wife Chava (Eve) and she conceived and gave birth to Cain". (Genesis 4:1) The use of the word *to know* for sex teaches that the image of God within man (or *tselem elokim*) demands a relationship based on knowledge and conscious purpose. To do otherwise is to mate through instinct as the animals do. Perhaps the key to the Jew's outstanding ability to create a people which is so successful in the areas of the intellect and the spirit, is the extreme care with which almost everyone in the Jewish community has guided the creation of new Jewish families.

SEX—A CONSTRUCTIVE FORCE

The Hebrew language, the Holy tongue, which possesses an inner logic and structure of its own, offers a valuable etymological insight to the religious view of the husband-wife relationship. The Hebrew words for man and woman are so formed that if we remove from the word "*Ish*", *Man*, and "*Ishah*", *Woman*, the letters "*yud*" and "*hay*", which form the name of God, what remains in each word are the two single letters "*alef*" and "*shin*", which spell the word "*Esh*" or fire. (Talmud: *Sotah* 17a)

This is more than a coincidence, since sex and fire share many striking similarities. Fire, together with the generation of light and heat, is a basic element of life and civilization, crucial to industry and manufacture. Employed correctly, fire is a constructive, essential, creative force, but when unattended and permitted to go out of control, fire will spread and destroy all in its path. This analogy applies to humans' use of their sexual faculties. When God is a partner in the relationship between a man and a woman, when the letters "*yud*" and "*hay*" remain, and if, therefore, God's laws govern a man and a woman joined together in a family *as one flesh*, sex is a constructive and positive force. Without God, *man* and *woman* lose control, sink to the level of the beast, and their relationship assumes the nature of "fire", with all its potentially negative, destructive, self-consuming and dangerous possibilities. For this reason, young people are cautioned not to *play with fire*. They may lose control and destroy not only their relationships, but themselves as well.

THE TRUE ROOTS OF LOVE

What is the real meaning of love? Where are the emotions and impulses that nourish and sustain it? There is hardly a person alive who does not harbor within himself or herself at least a spark of the unselfish impulse to give or to share. But since giving and sharing are possible only for people who are free to choose, it follows that only a person who *is* free to choose can give freely, voluntarily, and unselfishly enough to enjoy the fruits of a truly loving relationship. Moreover, one often discovers that the more he or she gives and the more he or she shares, the greater the return of satisfaction and joy that serves, in turn, to nourish, deepen, and sustain the person's love. Love, then, is a relationship notably dependent upon the mutual activities of giving and sharing.

Love in marriage flows from the fact that both husband and wife acknowledge the need for completion. A man is incomplete without a wife with whom he shares his life, home, children, and many other interests—while a woman is incomplete without a man who loves her and makes it possible for her to bear children, raise a family, and serve as the pivotal force of home, family, and community life. Each partner is therefore grateful to the other for the complementary role each plays, and such is the mutual giving and sharing that begets gratitude and a sense of oneness, twin foundations of a truly loving and successful marital relationship.

The relationship of husband and wife, with its core impulses of giving and loving, also reflects the selfless love of God for man. In fact, man's impulse to give may well derive from his own Godlikeness. Thus, the more a man and woman share, the more like God they may become. And the more they invest of time, effort, and concern for each other, the deeper, more stable, meaningful and secure will their relationship be.

God's relationship to man is based on His love for man. Since God is perfect, has no needs, and needs nothing in return, His love for man is completely selfless—it is based on giving without any anticipation of receiving.

The Hebrew word for love, "*Ahavah*", is related to the Aramaic word "*hav*", to give. To love is to give. True love is the product of giving to another individual. Love in its truest form is selfless; if it is self-serving or selfish it is not love at all.

He who gives, feels that part of himself is invested in the person of the recipient. There takes place a transference, since the recipient is no longer himself alone, but part of the giver. Each belongs to the other—committed to the other in a deep and lasting sense.

A person's heart is to be found where he or she has made his greatest investments. If a person's concern, time, and efforts are "invested" in husband, wife, and children, the love for them will increase and grow.

"*Chessed*", love and kindness, are among the basic elements and qualities of Jewish life. Love is the opposite of egotism and selfishness. It is a shift in the direction of one's concern from self to family—neighbors, community, and finally, the world at large. Marriage is the beginning of love because one is obligated to shift the focus of concern from self to husband, wife, and children. Therefore, one who refuses to marry is a person who denies one of the basic needs of being truly human: the need to feel for, live with, and love another person. As the Bible clearly warns: "It is not good for a person to live alone". (Genesis 2:18) To live alone is to deny the foundation of Jewish life, the emotion of love—*chessed*.

A person who does not marry becomes the last link in a chain that began with the first man and woman. When you do not bear children, the many qualities that make you a unique person die with you; you do not live on in the following generations. For this reason, those Jewish couples who are not blessed with children of their own make special efforts to become parents, in both a spiritual and physical sense, to children who lack parents. For the same reason, Jews reject the concept of celibacy, the idea that some great spiritual good can come from a life that lacks marriage, sharing, giving, and deep personal relationships—so deep that two people become one—and ultimately become like the *One*.

THE SIGNIFICANCE OF FAMILY

One of man's most basic responsibilities is to insure the continuity and immortality of self and mankind. But the act of bearing children is not a matter of physical survival alone. If a child is to fulfill the hopes of his parents, or more importantly, to satisfy the expectations of the Almighty, then man must procreate with a sense of purpose and responsibility. We are commanded, therefore, not only to bring children into the world in a biological sense, but also to rear children who will reflect the highest and best in ourselves, our families, our culture, and in Jewish society. Each child, furthermore, is a unique new personality, and should be encouraged and motivated to make his or her own mark and special contribution to the world-wide family of man.

The husband's and wife's task involves much more than bearing children. Their responsibility is to raise children who will be motivated to continue the tasks their parents have begun, but have left unfinished. Parents dream of raising children who will promote the tasks and preserve the treasures that preceeding generations have entrusted to their safekeeping, in the hope that they will not only preserve the treasures of the past, but will pass them on in an enriched and improved form.

The family is *the* instrument of Jewish continuity; it insures the Jewish future. Each generation is a link in a chain and, as such, is responsible and accountable to the generations which preceded it, as well as to those yet unborn. The family is the basic school of Jewish life. An appreciation of the significance of the family demands a sense of history and destiny. It calls for a deep understanding that each of us bears great responsibilities as a member of the family and of the Jewish nation. No one is an individual in his or her own right; no one has the right to say that his or her actions have no influence on the past, present, or future.

In the Jewish view, bringing a child into the world must be the result of thoughtful, mature, responsible action, performed in sanctity, by a couple who love and respect each other—who act in accordance with the laws set forth by God.

THE RIGHT TO LIFE

A brief mention of the Jewish position regarding abortion is significant at this point. Rabbi Israel Klavan, of blessed memory, then Executive Vice-President of the Rabbinical Council of America, was quoted in *Jewish Life*, March-April 1967:

> The unborn child, particularly after the 40th day of conception, has a right to life which cannot be denied him. Even if the fetus is the product of incest or rape, or an abnormality of any kind is foreseen, the right to life is still his...

The only condition under which this right may be denied is when it threatens the life of another, namely, the mother. Under the principle which permits taking the life of a human being in defense of another human being attacked by the first, an abortion can be permitted if the mother's life is endangered.

It is for a competent religious authority, upon consultation with medical authorities, to determine whether the threat to a mother's well-being is sufficient to warrant an abortion.

Each child has the right to life. Hopefully, it will be born into a family that will not only love and protect it, and provide for its material needs, but will also guide it and mold its personality. The family must literally "pour" itself into the child, because, in its earliest formative years, the family is its total environment. In order to do this properly, the family itself must have goals, ideals, purpose, and discipline. Even when a child is given over to others for brief periods, such as to a baby-sitter or a Day Care Center, care must be exercised to select these carefully, since early experiences can leave an indelible life-long impression.

WOMAN AS A "PERSON"

Woman is the key individual in the creation of the family. The role of the woman as wife, mother, teacher, and provider, the pivot and foundation of the family—and as a result, of all of society and history—requires that each woman fully appreciate the purpose of her sexuality and attractiveness and unique feminine personality.

The Jewish laws of family, sanctity and *tsnius*—modest behavior and dress—serve to protect the integrity of each person's personality and help to restrain each one from abusing his or her natural inclinations and drives. They help control sexual desires, in order to prevent these from dominating one's personality and conduct. Were such control absent, a person might also forget that his or her partner is at all times a person, created in God's image, deserving of respect and care; to be treated as one might expect him or herself to be treated. The Torah commands, "You shall love your fellow '*komocho*' (as yourself)" because he or she is, like *yourself*, created in God's image and entitled to the same treatment and consideration you would expect for yourself. Tragically, too many males look upon woman as a *thing*, an *it*, instead of as a *she*; as a means to physical self-gratification, instead of as a person.

As the result of the commercialized and projected images of sexually al-luring, stereotyped women, both on the screen and in print, men often come to regard women, without any compunction over the idea of ex-ploitation, solely as an instrument, a toy or a plaything to exploit and "have fun" with. The same, of course, applies to women who seduce men for their own selfish, personal or sexual purposes, without consider-ing how such conduct may affect their "partners". Some of us seem to think that the purpose of the opposite sex is solely to provide momentary pleasure, without responsibility and commitment, in complete disregard of the other person's needs or feelings. Men and women in our society often use and then discard one another like disposable objects. Jewish morality demands that we consider the needs of our partner, and not only our needs; and that we respect him or her as a human being endowed with dignity, divinity, and self-respect.

While there are some men who conceive of love as a type of conquest, of women as born to obey their commands, or as adornments, trophies, or prizes they can add to their collections, in the Jewish view women are full and equal partners, friends and companions, without whom life can never be complete or fulfilling. In addition, women are individuals with rights and duties which are not set arbitrarily by their husbands, but rather as defined by the laws of Torah. From the joyful union of men and wom-en comes all creation, from it should flow all of what is best in human society. Marriage, for this reason, is never merely a social contract, but rather, and more importantly, a holy bond and religious union, sanctified and blessed by God. The term for marriage in Hebrew, "*Kiddushin*", ho-liness, embraces an idea expressed quite effectively in the marriage service itself:

> Blessed are You...who has sanctified us with your command-ments and commanded us concerning illicit relations: You have forbidden to us those who are merely betrothed, and permitted us those who are married to us through consecrated wedlock. Blessed are You, O Lord, who sanctifies His people Israel through the marriage canopy, and the sanctification of marriage.

and later,

> Blessed are You, O Lord...who has created groom and bride,

joy and gladness, delight and cheer, love and harmony, peace and companionship...Blessed are You, O Lord, who makes the groom rejoice with the bride.

THE "PLAYBOY" IDEAL

Let us now compare this sublime Jewish view of woman with the secular contemporary approach, depicted in *Playboy, Penthouse,* and other similar magazines. Much of what is wrong with the "American attitude" towards sex and women can be traced to these trend-setting magazines. But to criticize *Playboy* and its many imitators that cater to both men and women, on the grounds of their provocativeness and obscenity, is to overlook the larger problem created by publications of this type. Their popularity and damaging influence cannot be attributed simply to their nude photographs. There are undoubtedly more titillating, erotic, seductive, and "better" sources of pornography and filth to be had for a price.

The greatest danger of these publications is in the attitudes and distorted values they have succeeded in injecting into American social attitudes— and the way they typify the inevitable result of all *"pritzus"* (breaking the rules of modesty and restraint). *Playboy*-type magazines are, in reality, anti-sexual in that they project sex as an accessory that can be used as a leisure-time activity, as a happy but mindless form of fun and recreation. These magazines are anti-woman in that woman is reduced to a male accessory, diluted and dissipated because she can be kept at a safe distance. Non-involvement is elevated to the ideal model for the *playboy*—women are no longer people to be respected, loved and cherished, but are converted into objects to be used as toys; playthings to be discarded when playtime is over. Similarly, *Playgirl*-type magazines, which cater to women, are anti-man. Pornography is anti-human because it reduces people to robots, ruled by their physical instincts, for whom life is a game that provides fun. Essentially, these magazines deny not only the dignity and freedom of the human spirit, but also the true and real natures of men and women themselves. Sex is far more complex, serious and significant than is self-deceptively and unrealistically admitted by popular American culture, which prefers to see it as fun and games for youthful recreation. Rollo May, the noted psychiatrist, has made the point in *Love and Will* that the women in *Playboy* seem not to be at all happy:

...as you look more closely you see a strange expression in

these photographed girls: detached, mechanical, uninviting, vac-
uous—the typical schizoid personality in the negative sense of
that term. You discover that they are not 'sexy' at all but that
'Playboy' has only shifted the fig leaf from the genitals to the
face.

Woman, as a person, is compromised and demeaned—all in marked
opposition to the attitude of the Torah, which views sex as part of a
healthy, permanent, workable "institution", in which woman is
protected and shares rights, duties, honors, and privileges with her
husband.

The popular pornographic magazines appeal to an alienated and spiritually deprived youth, who naively accept a terribly artificial image of what
it means to be a "man". For the uprooted young man or woman with
time on his or her hands and money in his or her pocket, these magazines
fill a special need. They are guidebooks to a glamorous world of false material values. They lure insecure young men, searching for their male
"identity" and for how to be a "man", by shrewdly feeding upon their
inexperience and gullibility. Many boys of all ages are looking for a dream,
and their imaginations and frustrations work overtime. Hugh Heffner
and his imitators have concocted all of these ingredients into a smashing
commerical success which tells the confused just what their immature
imaginations would like to hear.

In a world where the "in" thing means acquisition of the latest consumer product, sex is treated as just another item of leisure activity to be
handled with skill and detachment, like a car, a hi-fi set, a good pipe, or
drums. In fact, pornography is used as a tool to merchandise these items.
Women become desirable, even indispensable, as accessories to these objects—an "it" instead of a "she". This attitude reduces woman to a sym-
bol of sex on the animal level. Pornography teaches that sex must always
be contained within the sphere of entertainment and recreation. "Don't
complicate the cardinal principle of 'casualness and 'fun' by suggesting
marriage or any permanent relationship".

Unlike women in real life, the magazine readers' fictional girl-friend
stays comfortably uninvolved and distant, in her place, asking for nothing,
posing no threat and demanding nothing in terms of a permanent involvement or relationship. Like any good accessory, she is detachable and dis-
pensable. When playtime is over, the playmate's function ceases. She
must understand the rules of the game. When the young man is through

having "fun" with his favorite plaything, she can now be conveniently folded back into the centerfold. No responsibilities, goals or obligations—a make-believe world of sugar-coated nonsense. The female, in this case, is really no more than a prostitute, and color lithography has made it possible to turn our homes into artificial brothels by bringing the girls home in "literature" even small children are often permitted to see.

These magazines claim that their message is one of liberation, as they solemnly crusade for frankness and candor. Yet they, in fact, impose a new kind of tyranny, relegating life into a section of the consumer world and turning love into an idolatry of things in a materialistic world. They promote a bondage to things, and to people turned into things. The higher self of man is brought low, becoming enslaved to constant thoughts of passion, lust and desire. The mind becomes preoccupied with bodily desire, and its ability to refine the human motive and to purify its spirit is crippled in the process. The mystery and magic of human personality are reduced to a visual portrayal of females, who are superficial, paper-thin nobodies. The human in the person is debased, as the animal ruled by instinct takes over.

That there are young people who regularly fall for this abuse of their persons and personalities is not surprising, in light of the intense media and peer group pressure they are subjected to. Unfortunately, our entire directionless and uncontrolled system of dating, including the free exposure of boys and girls to each other on the dance floor, at the beach, and with the "gang", contribute to this sad situation, as do the pressures of style and the many social pressures to conform. To be *used* is to be prostituted. To be a *thing* is to cease to be human. To make a *game* of that emotion and powerful life-giving force which is the basis of the family and creates the next generation, is an insult to the human personality and a denial of a person's divinity and dignity.

DRESS AND CONDUCT

The most baffling and contradictory thing about some young women is their capacity to be forgetful of their own nature. The young woman who permits herself to be debased into becoming a "playmate" by dressing, dating, speaking or behaving in a blatantly seductive fashion is practicing self-deception, and is deceiving others as to her true character and nature. Not that every girl who veers from the highest standards of "*tsnius*" is consciously a "playmate". In most cases, she probably has no idea of what these standards are and is merely reacting to her environment and the social pressures of community, family and friends. But we would hope to have her realize that with every compromise she has taken a few more steps in that direction. It is troubling that many young women whose physical integrity, reputation and honor hang in the balance, should risk the fulfillment of their innermost dreams and drives to comply with social pressures or with the stubborn irresponsible urgings of an impetuous, impulsive young man. *His* grasp of the meaning of a family, children, a home and a future is, in comparison to the average young lady of his age, very immature. Often he is ready to "forget her" after he has "had his fun". Rarely is he honorable or responsible, for otherwise he would not dishonor someone else.

GUIDELINES OF DRESS AND CONDUCT FOR WOMEN

The Torah feels that a young woman who dresses or behaves in such a way that she is obviously advertising her body or blatantly flaunting her physical beauty is not only guilty of a conscious effort to seduce, but is responsible, as well, for the advances with which a young man will naturally respond and for the resultant compromises that may destroy her own reputation, physical integrity, and healthy sense of self-esteem. For when the sexual urgings of a young man are aroused, the honor of a young woman hangs precariously in the balance. He, on the one hand, may demand: "If you really love me how can you refuse"? While she, on the other hand, should be able to respond: "If you really love me, how could you ask?"

The obvious question we might ask is: why does love enter into this at all? Shouldn't the girl simply say: "If you respect me, you'd respect my principles"—or even further "Why don't you treat me as a person rather than as a mere object of desire"? The sexual attraction between man and woman is not a toy. Life, love, children, family and one's own posterity are too important to be fooled around with. Their place is in a blessed and permanent partnership, in a structure known as home and family.

These magazines and the media as a whole have created a moral climate which would lead us to believe that the sole aim and goal of life is pleasure and fun, a life where morality, responsibility, God, His Torah, its goals and ideals are "dead" issues. In truth, there is nothing new about the "new" morality. It is no different than the immorality of ancient Rome, the "sacred" prostitution of the Pagans, condemned by the prophets in the Bible, or the license, debauchery or hedonistic immorality practiced by many ancient pagan "religions". A close look at today's cults will reveal that much of the mental slavery they impose is through the controlled suppression or misuse of sex, much along the lines of ancient pagan cults which expected girls to serve as sacred Temple prostitutes for the sake of spreading the faith.

Jewish tradition expects a man to do much more than simply feed, clothe and protect his wife. He is to respect her, consult her, love her and hold her in esteem, no less than the way he expects to be treated by his wife. The Torah's commandment, "And you shall love your neighbor as you would want to be loved yourself", means above all that man must treat women precisely as he would want to be treated himself, and to follow strict Torah regulations that will never permit the compromise of a woman's body, dignity, integrity and future for the sake of a man's momentary pleasure or sexual gratification. Therefore, everything related to the urges, emotions, and organs associated with the sexual drive must be kept strictly within the confines of married life. By "everything", we necessarily mean *every* and *any* act of physical contact between the sexes, as well as the proper clothing or covering of the body of man and woman, in accordance with the *tsnius* standards set by Jewish law.

To quote Rabbi Joseph Grunblatt (*Jewish Life*, August, 1960):

> *Tsnius* is not an attempt to crush 'ugly sex,' but rather to reduce the frequency of stimuli which may lead to the improper use of sex; it is not a product of a fear or guilt complex, but an attempt to contain the sexual drive at its natural level.

The human body is beautiful, but, what is more important, *it is holy*. Sex is good, but only at the correct time and place and only with the person to whom one is married.

ANOTHER VIEW OF PORNOGRAPHY

Let us consider another aspect of the popular pornographic literature that has become so accepted in many circles of American society. The magazine stands of America are flooded each month with a new supply of slick, luxuriously printed, full-color pornographic magazines whose dominant feature is their suggestive photos of unclothed women. All pretenses at culture or literature aside, the front cover of any of these monthlies is ample proof that they are purchased principally for their pornography.

There are men who own stacks of back copies of these magazines. How are we to understand the rush to buy each month's new issue? Wouldn't it be sufficient to "review" a few past issues? Do the girls in this month's *Playboy* have anything that has not been seen in last month's issue, or in the issues of the past few years? Since by now these magazines leave nothing to the imagination, and there are no new surprises, what are the purchasers of *Playboy*, etc., looking for month after month?

In my opinion, the answer might be as follows: Each man instinctively believes that there is at least *one* special woman who will make him "happy". The men who regularly purchase these magazines are pursuing a grand illusion. They anticipate that this month they will finally see the unique, special girl who will bring them true happiness. If a man's vision of women and beauty is mostly physical, if he has been taught that happiness is brought about through physical, material things and external features, is it farfetched for this man to hope, at least subconsciously, that from among the new girls in this month's issue of his favorite pornographic magazine, he will find that special girl, with just those unique physical features, who will bring him bliss? If America's vision of beauty is skin deep, it might as well be paper thin.

Of course, mature people will readily acknowledge that it is a childish illusion to think that happiness is available from more or less flesh here or there, or that a particular physical feature seen on the printed page, or even in the flesh of someone we are close to, will affect our relationship or state of happiness. Even the readers of *Playboy* I'm sure, will agree. But remember, we are talking about an illusion; the *subconscious* motive for buying this month's issue.

Human beings are much more than the illusion, or even the reality of beauty. We are complicated, sensitive, intricate, complex and multifaceted; we are unique beings, created in God's image. We are personality, soul and spirit. Despite occasional appearances, or some contrary opinions, we are much more than sophisticated animals.

WHAT SHOULD WE REVEAL?

If we give human uniqueness some thought we, will agree that *uniqueness* in man or woman is basically to be found in their features from the neck up.

From the neck down individuals of the same sex are rather much the same. The part of our bodies that sets us apart from one another is the head—the part we generally reveal. The parts that are primarily animal-like, and *do not reflect the unique aspects* of the human personality, are parts we generally conceal. Jewish morality strongly urges that we cover our animal-like parts, and reveal only those features which reflect the unique aspects of our personalities; our eyes, mouth, ears, face and hands. The features and functions of men and women below the neck, such as reproduction, digestion, elimination and motion are, in appearance and in function, remarkably similar to those of the animals in that they are not expressions of our uniqueness.

We recognize people when we see their heads and faces; if we cover a person's face and look at the remainder of their body unclothed, we would probably not be able to recognize anyone. Maybe this helps explain why even the most modest or pious never suggest that animals cover their bodies or reproductive organs. An animal is a creature of instinct, a slave to its biology; it reacts to stimuli and lacks freedom of choice. Animals mate when their instinct compels them to mate. Since they are incapable of free choice or creativity, their bodily functions are often performed in the open, without any sense of shame. A cow has no need to conceal her sexual organs because a cow has nothing unique to conceal. A cow is all instinct, all body—from head to hoof. *A cow has no need to conceal her body because she lacks the need to reveal any aspects of herself.* Human beings conceal their animal-like features in order to allow their unique, God-like features to attract and to interact.

THE MYSTERY OF THE HUMAN FACE

How do people differ? The uniqueness of man and woman is revealed by their faces. When one observes the faces of one's friends, it is quite obvious that each is uniquely different. In this obvious way, God has imprinted His stamp and seal on each human being. He has demonstrated that even though there are billions of men and women on earth, each person is uniquely different; each is created in the "image", or reflection of God.

Analyzed element by element, the variables of the human face are limited. How many differently shaped noses are there? How different are lips or cheeks? The eyes are an excellent example. From the pictures of people in a magazine, cut out the eyes of a hundred people. Do they look much different one from the other? Yet, when we speak of a beautiful person, we often refer to the eyes, because the eyes have that unique ability to mirror the soul and to reflect the inner self.

Despite the limited number of variables in the physical features of the human face, the number of *different* human faces in the world is infinite. No two people are alike—each is uniquely different. Each human face is a reflection of God, who is infinite and unique and who endows mankind, His special creation, with a unique personality.

Unlike the English word *face*, which describes man's external physical features, the Hebrew word for face, *"panim"*, literally means *"inside"*. This indicates that the Torah views the face as a mirror of the unique qualities which make up human personality. The human face is where the personality is reflected—the face mysteriously combines the physical-biological, the personality-soul, the inner quality of each person.

The mystery of the human face is an even greater miracle when we realize that mankind originated from one father, Adam, and from one mother, Eve. Each human being is stamped from the mold of one father and mother. Unlike a coin mold which always turns out a precise replica, the human "mold" always turns out a new human being who is uniquely different. This follows from the fact that the first human being was one and unique. This quality of uniqueness, and the evidence that our spiritual and physical father is one and unique, is still very much with us, no matter how many human beings there are or will be born into the world.

To quote the Talmud (Sanhedrin 4:5) "Flesh and blood is minted into many coins with one mold; all resemble one another, and the Holy One, blessed be He, mints every person with the mold of the First Man. Yet no one resembles another". This is the true source of the uniqueness and singularity of man. From this we see that the fact of "man having been created single" is the source for two fundamental human principles, the unity of mankind and the uniqueness of every human being. (For a full and comprehensive understanding of the concepts of human unity and uniqueness, as well as the commandment to "love others as we love ourselves", see the lecture by Rabbi Yitschok Hutner, zts"l, in *Pachad Yitzchok*, Volume *Shavuos*, Chapter 21, translated in the Fall 1975 issue of *Tradition*.)

The Bible describes Moses' face following the giving of the Torah on Mt. Sinai by telling us that "the people were unable to look at him because the flesh of his face was radiant". Anyone who has been in the presence of a truly great rabbi or *tsaddik* knows that he has seen a unique and

God-like face that radiates the greatness of personality and the sanctity of the Torah he personifies. If you want to "*see* God" in this world, look into the face of a great rabbi.

Because the face reflects the Godly in Man, its features relate most directly to man's ability to choose between good and evil. All of the functions of the face—thinking, speaking, seeing, discerning, hearing and eating—relate to our ability to choose. The Jew even eats in a way that reflects choice and Godliness, which is one possible reason for the laws of kashruth.

We do not conceal our faces because they reflect our unique God-like personalities. We conceal our bodies because they reflect our animal-like features. Mature young people must be careful to be attractive to each other through those aspects of themselves which are God-like and unique, not through their animal-like features which should be modestly clothed. A young woman who must resort to exposing herself in order to win friends too often finds that her "friends" want her for her body but not for herself.

By keeping our bodies covered, we remove our more erotic features from the process of interpersonal relations. We attract each other not through the "instinct" aspects of our bodies, but through those features which make us unique and God-like. Let the animal in us be controlled by conscious free-will choice, so that we will not be overwhelmed and enslaved by the attractiveness of our animal-like features. *If the unique in me is attracted to that which is unique in the person of the other sex—chances are that our relationship will be unique and lasting. If the God-like in me attracts that which is God-like in that person, chances are that our relationship will contain elements of holiness and eternity.*

Since the exposure of the body heightens the degree of physical self-awareness, clothing the body helps heighten spiritual self-awareness. The covering of the body does not imply that the body is sinful; on the contrary, it affirms that the body is holy.

The Holy of Holies in Solomon's Temple in Jerusalem contained the Golden Ark of the Covenant in which were kept the stone tablets of the Ten Commandments. The Golden Ark was an exquisite work of art, beautifully sculptured; yet it was kept concealed in the Holy of Holies behind heavy drapes. Only the High Priest was permitted to enter the Holy of Holies, and then only once a year—on Yom Kippur. The ark was concealed because its physical beauty was but the carrier of its spiritual essence. It was kept hidden to prevent one from being diverted from its spiritual essence by the glitter of its art and gold. One can be easily overwhelmed by one's visual senses and diverted from more essential aspects not easily apprehended by the senses. When a person emphasizes the physical and overwhelms the senses, he or she cannot focus on the spiritual.

THE JEWISH CONCEPT OF HEROISM

The Jews and Western Civilization often differ quite substantially concerning the fundamental nature of human achievement, bravery and heroism. To the Jew, the greatest and most important accomplishments are generally those which we do privately, in secret, accompanied by an attitude of humility, reserve and modesty; to the non-Jew, accomplishment and heroic behavior generally call for public display, publicity and open public acclaim.

The ancient Greeks turned physical beauty into an object of worship. Their gods were statues of marble and gold. They actually worshipped their heroes and celebrated heroic achievement with public tributes, stage plays, temple monuments, hymns and songs. Their greatest accomplishments were the heroic acts of soldiers and sportsmen on the battlefield and in the stadium. The Greek concept of perfection was directly related to those things which could be shown to the human eye or perceived by the senses.

To the Jew, the highest accomplishment lies in the refinement of human character and the perfection of human personality; in the educating, shaping, molding, disciplining and elevating of each self, and ultimately all of human society. Rabbi Ben Zoma (Pirkei Avot 4:1) taught: "Who is strong? He who subdues his passions. For it is written: 'Greater is the person who rules over his personality and spirit than he who has conquered a city.'" A person who manages to control his or her desires rather than allowing them to control him or her is one who has achieved true greatness.

Maybe this explains why the Greeks, Romans, and Egyptians—all the great civilizations of the ancient world—ultimately disappeared from the stage of history, while the Jew miraculously survives, thrives and marches on despite the efforts of so many powerful nations, from ancient times up to our day, to destroy him.

Each culture and each nation in the world strives for perfection in its own way, some in art, music, architecture, drama, and literature, some in the arts of war and business. At some point each society reaches its apex and arrives at a pinnacle of achievement. A feeling then overtakes that society that it has reached its full potential and has arrived at the heights of accomplishment. A society which is creative in music, art, and literature begins at some point to feel that it has achieved "perfection" and can go no further. Once a society feels that it has exhausted its creative impulse, it loses the drive to overcome its internal and external enemies. Inwardly that society behaves as though there is nothing more to accomplish.

In the process of achieving perfection in the cultural and material realm, a process of despair and aimlessness wreaks havoc on the individual and the family, leading to increased crime and corruption. Lacking a firm code of morality, ethics and humanity, such a society collapses of its own weight or of its inability to withstand the onslaught of its enemies. It no longer has the will to fight or live, because life has lost its meaning. Soon it is overwhelmed by another, more powerful society whose armies pulverize its demoralized defenses and the cycle begins all over again.

The Jew is not subject to this cyclic process of the rise and fall of societies and civilizations. The Jew lives on, sometimes in the Land of Israel, and at times in exile, without the land. Jewish life continues whether the Temple is standing or is destroyed, as a nation of few or many, persecuted or tolerated. The Jew has survived destruction, exile, pogrom and holocaust to emerge again and again, generation after generation, surviving civilization after civilization, only to reemerge and again to continue the long chain of tradition by producing new generations of great thinkers, rabbis and teachers. This is because Jewish creativity seeks the perfection of man, his spirit, and personality. The Jew continues the struggle until ultimately human society and human civilization will be perfected. Whatever his condition, the Jew gives priority to personality and family. No matter how downtrodden, the Jew continues to survive with the faith that in the end of days the people which does God's will shall inherit God's world. The Jew believes that one day "the Lord will be King over all the earth" and that all of mankind will fully accept His Kingdom.

In the Jewish world, the great accomplishments of life are often done in private, in the home where no one sees, in the privacy of one's own heart and mind, where moral strength and determination, coupled with an ability to turn one's back on the ever-present temptation of sin and lust, are private battles waged and won within. The ability to say "no" to sin, lust, and temptation is an achievement performed in secret. The private heroism of the individual is most precious to God, who sees and knows the secrets of the heart, and who rewards His true heroes.

A unique aspect of *tsnius* is the idea that who I am is ultimately a private affair. My relationship with God, the ultimate source of reality, is something which no other human being can really share. No one else but God knows all of my secret thoughts and aspirations. In Judaism, therefore, the greatest heroic acts were performed in private.

A few examples:

•Abraham is told to sacrifice his beloved only son, Isaac, whom he sees as his heir. He takes him to Mt. Moriah and does as God commands him. God was but testing him and did not actually want him to sacrifice his son. This act of devotion is done in complete isolation. No one is there to observe it.

•Jacob wrestles with the Angel of God. This is a struggle which determines the future direction of the Jewish people. After the battle, he is no longer *Jacob*, the downtrodden. Now he is renamed *Israel*, the Prince. This battle and the ultimate victory take place in the dead of night with no one else present. Jacob is alone with no one to encourage him and no one to witness his struggle.

•When Moses first confronts God at the Burning Bush, he, too, is alone. Later, following the revelation of the Ten Commandments before the entire Jewish people, Moses goes up to Mt. Sinai to receive the remainder of the Torah. God warns him to go alone. No one else observes the greatest act of communication between man and God. Later, when Moses communicates with God on a regular basis in the *Mishkan*, the Tabernacle, he goes alone.

•Each Yom Kippur, the holiest day of the year, the High Priest entered the Holy of Holies in the Temple to obtain forgiveness for the sins of the entire Jewish people. At the most crucial moment of that ceremony, he disappears behind a partition and worships alone. No one is there to observe him.

Inwardness and privacy, which personify all Jewish ideals, relate in a special way to the life of the Jewish woman.

Now we can understand what the Psalms (45:14) mean when they say that, *"Kol K'vodah Bas-Melech Pe'nimah"*—the entire glory and grandeur of the King's daughter is the expression of her inner qualities. "Though the princess may appear glorious and splendid in public, she reveals her true glory in womanly virtue only in quiet, more private circles, and the splendid qualities she shows there are much greater than the exquisite beauty of the gold borders which shine at the hems of her garments''. (Hirsch, Psalms)

It is for the above reasons that we pursue *tsnius*, privacy and modesty in behavior and dress, and believe that pornography dehumanizes and denigrates the human being. It is for these reasons too, that we emphasize that the pursuit of *tsnius*, modesty and privacy, promotes happiness and realism in human relations, while the encouragement of pornography and sexual "freedom" is the pursuit of an illusion at best, and human misery and disillusion at its worst.

SEX EDUCATION

In the Jewish world of Europe, *tsnius* (inwardness-privacy) was learned not only from holy books, but from the entire Jewish environment, which was a living example of *tsnius*. *Tsnius* existed not only in the home, but in the Jewish street as well. A Jew could learn *tsnius* by studying his mother, father, teachers and friends with the same intensity that we search for Torah truths in books. Jewish youth in the classical Jewish society learned even more from *source people* than from source books. Jewish youth absorbed at an early age the living example of their elders' way of life, which was the real reflection of their greatness in Torah. Jewish youth could readily see how hard they had to work, how high the stakes were and how much energy was required for every breakthrough in personality growth, for every improvement of the *neshomoh*, soul. Even in that protected environment, saturated with holiness, each individual was aware of the tension which exists between the soul and the inner force which pulls toward evil—the *yetser horah*. In molding his personality, the Jew viewed himself as though he were a lion-tamer in a cage with a wild beast. Every action, every motion, every gesture had to be measured with microscopic precision—lest the beast become bold and strike.

What is most interesting about classical-traditional Jewish societies is that sex education was not acquired by Jewish youth from the gutter, from movies or smutty books. The family relationship is openly and frankly discussed in the *Chumash*, in the books of the Bible, in the *Mishna* and in the *Talmud*. It was and is by no means unusual for a boy of thirteen or fourteen to study the Talmudic books of *Nidah* (the menstruating woman), and the laws of holiness that relate to *Gittin* (divorce), or *Kiddushin* (marriage—literally sanctification). Nor do these books pull punches or hide behind subterfuge. Jewish youth learned the "facts of life" in the Jewish school, in an atmosphere of discipline and holiness, rather than from smutty jokes, or obscene books secretly passed around.

But Jewish "sex education" is not clinical biology, taught cynically by secular teachers who themselves lack definite moral standards. It is taught simply, frankly, with full reverence for the mysteries and sanctities of love and life, with the realization that the world of a married couple is a sacred trust that must never be taken lightly. Jewish youth were never ignorant, shocked or terrified by the "facts", they never had to turn to the streets for their initiation, because the "facts" were part of the life of a *holy people*, and were presented clearly and straightforwardly in the Bible and in the sacred texts.

4
The Deeper Meaning of Human Sexuality

We all instinctively sense that *sin*, with a capital *S*, as distinguished from *crime*—theft, bribery, murder, libel—and other evil, relates in some way to the area of unsanctioned sex. The reasons are quite simple. Sex is the one area of temptation that is ever present, most obvious and most common. Few of us are tempted to steal our neighbor's coat or wallet, but every so often a man is tempted to lust after his neighbor's wife, or to misbehave with a pretty girl with whom he has nothing at all in common except that she is pretty and, he hopes, "common".

Sex also plays tricks on our sense of values. On the one hand, we say to ourselves, "What does it matter what I do"? After all, "if I *steal a kiss*, I've really stolen nothing". Or we might rationalize that sex is just a physical or biological function, much like eating. On the other hand, when a man is all consumed with infatuation or desire, he may talk himself into thinking that his infatuation is *the* most important thing and he will not rest until he has conquered the object of his desire, so that the infatuation or desire seems to fill all of his thoughts, pushing everything else to the side. It is no wonder that man's greatest desire, the urge he must learn to control most, is linked to his greatest act of creativity, his most significant

43

partnership with the Eternal and Divine—the task of creating new human life and of sharing with God the function of being the world's *Creator*.

In its purely physical aspects, sex seems to be no less a part of our natural functions than digestion or breathing. And that is precisely its greatest danger—that we may be tempted not to exercise self-control, or, by using our power to rationalize, we will think of it as a natural function over which we need exercise no special restraint. Thus we may be tempted to act as do the animals, who copulate as freely as they eat, whenever the urge or desire takes hold of them, without "human" considerations—out in the open, without shame, modesty, ceremony or formality. One who acts this way, though, forgets that, unlike digestion or breathing, sex involves *two* people.

If, in fact, sex could remain "pure", meaning purely animal, instinctive and automatic, like other functions of the human body, then the *evil inclination* would have nothing to do with it. We all know that sex is much more than this; that it is strongly linked to love, to the spirit, to the core of our personality and self-image, to the institutions of family and procreation. Its physical aspects create deep emotional involvements and relationships. We know too, how closely sex is associated with guilt, with conscience, with our sensitivity to right and wrong. Even beyond this, it is linked to our instinctive desire to live on into eternity through our children.

While sexual intercourse is a mutual, shared event, it is, at least in the purely physical sense, something a man does *to* a woman as well as with a woman. The woman's very being has been changed by an outside force. The woman is the recipient, the woman has been penetrated by an outsider who has entered her body. No longer is she only herself. The man remains biologically unaffected, in that nothing has happened to his body, but the woman is affected much more profoundly than the man, now she has part of *him* in *her*, unless of course this has been blocked through the use of a birth prevention device. And if she conceives as a result of this union, her life would be changed permanently. Perhaps this explains why a young woman, even when she mates thoughtlessly and irresponsibly with a person to whom she is not married, may be overtaken by a deep felt instinctive emotion that she is now "his girl". In some mystical sense, she feels possessed. She *belongs* to him. While other factors may, in time, override and erase this emotion, the feminine feeling that one act of intimacy creates a permanent bond is deeply imbedded in the human psyche.

On a second level, sex differs from other natural functions in that it is voluntary, and lacks urgency and necessity. In other words, it is a physical function which, more than any other, can be controlled by the mind and the will. It is, for example, necessary to breathe, and for the heart to beat. These are involuntary functions, in that no amount of self control can delay them. Extended abstention from food and drink will ultimately result in death from thirst or starvation, but it is possible to live for many years entirely celibate without physical harm. Sex, while a physical bodily function, is ruled by the will. We are free to use it or not to use it, but its use requires a conscious free-will decision.

Sex is so closely associated with sin precisely because we can freely choose how and when to use it. Sex relates most to the one area in which man resembles God—the area of "freedom of choice", the capacity to exercise free will. Furthermore, sex is essential to the highest form of human creativity. All humans share God's function as the Creator through their ability to create children, to bring about further generations of men and women. Precisely because our sexual drive is linked to freedom of choice and human creativity, its abuse is potentially so harmful. Uncontrolled, our sexual drives can twist our freedom, overpower our mind and will, pervert our creativity, and lead us to actions not in our best interest. Sex becomes harmful only when our bodily desire takes control, leaving our mind and will out of the picture. Uncontrolled, sexual desire can pervert the act of love, make it impersonal, or turn it into an obsession.

THE "NEW" MORALITY

Our generation has learned that by freeing people from repression and guilt—that is, from discipline, control, and recognition of right or wrong—we are not healthier emotionally.

What are the results of removing restraint and controls, and introducing a "New Morality" of sexual "freedom" and license? Modern man and woman often find that sex without restraints makes sex boring, insignificant and meaningless. Such sex may release physical tensions, but it never assumes a higher level of emotional and spiritual significance beyond that of children's kissing games. This is the kind of sex that dehumanizes us by turning us into robots, degrading one of the most precious of human gifts—the ability to love. Dr. Rollo May, one of America's leading psychotherapists describes the "impotence, emptiness, meaninglessness" of what should be "the most intimate, loving, fulfilling of acts" in his *Love and Will* (pages 39–42):

> In Victorian times, when the denial of sexual impulses, feelings, and drives was the mode and one would not talk about sex in polite company, an aura of sanctifying repulsiveness surrounded the whole topic. Males and females dealt with each other as though neither possessed sexual organs. William James, that redoubtable crusader who was far ahead of his time on every other topic, treated sex with the polite aversion characteristic of the turn of the century. In the whole two volumes of his epoch-making *Principles of Psychology*, only one page is devoted to sex, at the end of which he adds "These details are a little unpleasant to discuss...."
>
> Then, in the 1920's, a radical change occurred almost overnight. The belief became a militant dogma in liberal circles that the opposite of repression—namely, sex education, freedom of talking, feeling, and expression—would have healthy effects, and obviously constituted the only stand for the enlightened person. In an amazingly short period following World War I, we shifted from acting as though sex did not exist at all to being obsessed with it. We now placed more emphasis on sex than any society since that of ancient Rome, and some scholars believe we are more preoccupied with sex than any other people in all of history. Today, far from not talking about sex, we might well seem, to a visitor from Mars dropping into Times Square, to have no other topic of communication.
>
> ...Open any newspaper, any day (Sunday in particular), and the odds are you will find some pundit treating the public to his views on contraception, abortion, adultery, obscene publications, homosexuality between consenting adults or (if all else fails) contemporary moral patterns among our adolescents.
>
> ...Partly as a result of this radical shift, many therapists today rarely see patients who exhibit repression of sex in the manner of Freud's pre-World War I hysterical patients. In fact, we find in the people who come for help just the opposite: a great deal of talk about sex, a great deal of sexual activity, practically no one complaining of cultural prohibitions over going to bed as often or with as many partners as one wishes. But what our patients do complain of is lack of feeling and passion. The curi-

ous thing about this ferment of discussion is how little anyone seems to be *enjoying* emancipation. So much sex and so little meaning or even fun in it.

...But *internal* anxiety and guilt have increased. And in some ways these are more moribund, harder to handle, and impose a heavier burden upon the individual than external anxiety and guilt.

...College students, in their fights with college authorities about hours girls are to be permitted in the men's rooms, are curiously blind to the fact that rules are often a boon. Rules give the student time to find himself. He has the leeway to consider a way of behaving without being committed before he is ready.... Better to have the lack of commitment direct and open rather than to go into sexual relations under pressure—doing violence to his feelings by having physical commitment without psychological. He may flout the rules; but at least they give some structure to be flouted.

...What we did not see in our short-sighted liberalism in sex was that throwing the individual into an unbounded and empty sea of free choice does not in itself give freedom, but is more apt to increase inner conflict. The sexual freedom to which we were devoted fell short of being fully human.

...Our "dogmatic enlightenment" is self-defeating: it ends up destroying the very sexual passion it set out to protect. In the great tide of realistic chronicling, we forgot, on the stage and in the novel and even in psychotherapy, that imagination is the life-blood of eros...Indeed, there is nothing *less* sexy than sheer nakedness, as a random hour at any nudist camp will prove. It requires the infusion of the imagination...to transmute physiology and anatomy into *interpersonal* experience....

WHEN SEX IS PERVERTED

In the early years of the Israeli kibbutz collective farm movement, boys and girls born in certain *kibbutzim* affiliated with the extreme left wing *Mapam* movement, lived, ate, and slept in the same quarters, dressing and showering together. These *kibbutzim* advocated free love and destruction of the family and the old morality in accordance with Marxist dogma.

These extreme practices were eventually discontinued because the children born to these couples were often emotionally confused and disturbed.

When these young people married, their social and sexual interests were far from normal and acceptable. For one thing, they hardly ever married amongst each other. The result was the perversion of healthy and natural impulses, because they never developed normal reactions to sexual impulses.

Similar social breakdowns developed among their free-loving parents. *Kibbutz* men decided after a while that, no matter how committed they were in principle to the concept of free love, they simply wouldn't tolerate seeing "their woman" go off to sleep with other men. In fact, in a number of instances, men were so consumed and blinded by jealousy and anger that they actually lashed out and murdered their neighboring rivals. The leaders of these *kibbutzim* finally conceded that without some form of legal marriage and a stable family structure, no peaceful human society of any kind could exist, not to speak of the ideal society they envisioned. Sociological studies of other cultures which practiced "free love" family arrangements reveal similar problems. The concept might seem perfect on paper, but it simply doesn't work.

NUDITY

Normal responses to normal impulses are subverted, too, in a nudist-camp type of arrangement, where men and women discover after the first ten minutes of walking around in a state of complete undress that they are already losing a natural sense of body awareness and are already failing to be stimulated sexually in the presence of other totally defrocked men or women parading about. People who shed their clothing in this way divest themselves at the same time of a sense of self-respect, dignity, and private identity. In addition, sexual union for these people becomes often, of necessity, reduced to a purely physical, mechanical, and bodily act. For, where nothing has been hidden, there is no mystique, no romance, no prelude to the possibility for a natural 'act of love'.

By taking off one's clothes one doesn't become more human, but less so. God in his wisdom created man and woman with their many differences, their attractions, and their sexual stimulations so that they might rise above the animal, and not sink to the level of animals who live together like chickens and roosters.

Not only is our sexuality depressed, our very humanity, self-respect and dignity are depressed. Reducing "love" to the pursuit of bodily pleasure takes romance and sanctity out of life. Sex becomes an animal function rather than an expression of love and devotion.

What is meant when we say that man was created in the "image" or "likeness of God"? To the extent that a person does that which the animal is incapable of doing—he achieves the image of God. The wearing of clothes, the practice of modesty, the restraint of passion and instinct—that is the image of God.

THE ROLE OF TSNIUS IN A HEALTHY SEXUAL RELATIONSHIP

Once nakedness becomes mundane and a self-conscious attitude toward sex is abandoned—men and women cease to be sexually stimulated. It is therefore the purpose of *tsnius*, with its concept of modesty in conduct and dress, not simply to confine and restrict sexual stimulation and activity to the parameters of marriage, but also to help keep alive the interest of men in women and women in men in general. Boredom, disinterest, and perversion, infidelity and divorce, therefore, were very seldom problem areas in Jewish communities where the laws of *tsnius* were taught, lived, and genuinely respected.

A NEW FEMINIST ATTITUDE TOWARD DRESS

In the contemporary age of promiscuity and swinging liberation, a new type of woman has emerged. She burns her bra and reveals her breasts not to entice, but rather to assert her independence and to insist that sex and body are of no interest or significance to her at all. Her body bared as a matter of fact is helping her to make a statement: "I will dress as I choose. I will not be inhibited by any meaningless mores of society. I will not be exploited as a sex object or used for the pleasure of any chauvinist male. What I am displaying is simply skin and nothing that should bother or stimulate a man in any way. He will soon regard me *as a person, not as a female*".

Unfortunately, though, such women are simply trying to deny a fact of life. . . because there *are* differences between male and female and there *will always continue to be* differences between male and female. And the efforts of any woman to defy or to rebel against traditional concepts of modesty and morality will not serve to make her more human, but only less. The most human people, after all, are those who accept the reality of what they are and who relate to their fellow human beings with a genuine sense of awareness and understanding.

5
Youth:
Launching Pad for
Adulthood

FRIENDSHIP BEFORE MARRIAGE

Why *does* Jewish Tradition demand that the relationship between men and women before marriage stop at the point of physical contact? And why is such restraint, forbidding even mere "touching" (or *negiah* in Hebrew), so crucial a factor in the successful observance of those laws that define the Jewish standards of family loyalty and sanctified existence?

Jewish law states that once a young woman begins menstruating, she assumes the status of *nidah*, and remains, from that point on, "off limits", in regard to physical contact with men, until the day of her marriage. Just prior to her marriage ceremony she removes the *nidah* status, in accordance with Torah law, by immersing herself in the waters of a *mikveh* (a body of water used *only for spiritual sanctification*), and may then be approached by her husband as a partner in sexual union. As a married woman she becomes *nidah* once again with each onset of a menstrual period, and marital relations must then be suspended until she immerses herself, once more, in a *mikveh*, at least one week after the completion of each menstrual period.

It will be acknowledged, even by those unaware of this law, that the sense of touch in male-female relationships often constitutes a type of borderline where simple association begins to pass from the area of friendship into the area of intimacy and sex. In any male-female relationship, it is easier to maintain self control up to the point of physical contact because, from the moment of contact on, control becomes much more difficult. Also, once the principle of 'no contact' has been violated, there are often no other barriers effective enough in helping two people to restrain themselves from further kinds of involvement that could lead naturally to a final act of union or sexual consummation.

Just as a physical relationship is an essential element in the binding together of two people in marriage, no less, before marriage, does physical contact of any kind have the effect of forging bonds, of distorting objectivity and of introducing temptations with which most people find themselves unable to cope. Any sort of physical contact or intimacy, as it brings people closer together, tends to bind—a kind of glue as it were—but as glue should be used to *bind* together *only* when a permanent bond is decided upon, physical contact should begin only after the marriage itself has been formalized.

"Therefore shall a man leave his father and his mother and *cleave* (from the root word *devek*, or binding force, and hence the idea of glue itself) to his *wife*, and they shall become one flesh" (Genesis 2:24). The Torah used the above analogy when it described the physical relationship in terms of a sort of glue that binds one person to another.

Some young Americans will claim, with reasonable justification, that some of the social practices which *Halachah* (Jewish law) prohibits, such as hand holding, social dancing, and good-night kissing, are simply matters of form or social grace, which young people perform without attaching to them any great significance.

It is just this point that we are attempting to make. As Jews, we take relationships between people much more seriously than does "society". Jewish society cannot tolerate a situation where a young woman, or a young man lets her or himself be used, taken advantage of, or hurt. Nor can we accept, for all the casualness of American youth, that kissing, or any form of expressing affection, can ever be regarded lightheartedly or as a game or social grace.

Most young people who have been involved in the dating situation know that even a casual good-night kiss can be just a beginning. The nature of kissing and touching is such that it usually calls for more and more...once you begin, it is hard to stop. If each date begins with the understanding that before it ends there must be some kind of physical contact or sexual expression, then the high point of the date is the physical contact or sexual expression, and not a more intellectual or conversational type of exchange, or the excitement of sharing each other's company. If dating is limited to conversation, then each successive date can bring new and more stimulating conversation, and a greater interplay of personality. But if dating implies sex, *even* the most casual sex, it is natural that on each date you will want to have more or better sex; each partner will feel impelled to give a little more, to let down a few more barriers, until there is little left to surrender. The end result is that the young woman pays with her body for dates or for some *progress* in the relationship. The result is a transaction in which the young woman is selling herself cheaply and all too often suffers a loss of self-respect, self-worth, self-esteem, and in many instances the breaking of the relationship.

BETWEEN ENGAGEMENT AND MARRIAGE

If a young man and woman have decided definitely to marry and have become formally engaged, do they violate any *Halachic* prohibition by the start, at that point, of a sexual relationship? A number of matters should be discussed in response to the above question.

First, the opening blessing of a Jewish marriage ceremony explains that a young man and woman, even though engaged, are still prohibited from consummating their relationship in the sexual act. Why? Perhaps because too many engagements are broken when partners begin to discover, at closer range, that they may not be quite as ideally suited for marriage with each other as they had originally thought. And because, as difficult, tense, and complicated as it is to break an ordinary engagement, it becomes even more difficult and emotionally devastating to dissolve a bond where sex has been part of the relationship. According to Jewish tradition, therefore (among other reasons), in order to protect a young man or woman from unnecessary grief or emotional harm, it is only the formal marriage ceremony that can establish the legality and permissibility of sexual union.

Then, too, since the bond between a man and woman is not simply a permit for living together but rather a holy institution, and if marriage requires sanctification and the blessing of God, a Jew who is committed to the disciplined life of *halachah* will act only after the ceremony of sanctification has been officially performed. Jewish ritual specifies that whenever a blessing (or *brocha*) for any act is to be recited, it is recited *before* the act is performed. Where a young man and woman feel they cannot wait, by all means they should marry sooner, but they should not make a mockery of the wedding ceremony by performing the act first and reciting the blessing after.

"Why", one might ask, "must the Torah set a *single standard* for behavior when in each case a completely different set of personalities and circumstances is involved"? It is precisely because each individual has a different threshold of stimulation and tolerance for restraint that the Torah must establish a firm and universal ruling in this area. Sex is too potent a force and too vital a factor in determining the success of married life to be treated casually, or to be permitted free and unrestrained expression. Sex outside of marriage often leads to complications of involvement that may result in greater degrees of frustration, fear, insecurity, depression, or despair than any temporary benefit, satisfaction, or feeling of fulfillment can possibly ever justify.

The Torah seeks, therefore, as does any code of law or system of government, to establish basic uniform standards that will apply to every member of its society for the greater good of all. Therefore, when the Torah says "NO SEX" to an individual, the law protects all members of society. No single moment of pleasure, according to Jewish tradition, is worth the pain of guilt, tragedy, or even simple unhappiness that it might cause or inflict upon another.

We all know that no sustained physical relationship remains stationary. Sex may contain elements of "fun", but to limit it to that function alone is deceptive. That approach either leads to complicated involvements and conflicts or, in the end, causes it to cease to be fun. Surprisingly, sex can become a disgusting drag, a burden that brings despair, a complex of frustration, fear, insecurity and personal unhappiness.

The Torah's rules apply the brakes before the car begins to roll down the hill creating a lifetime of misery and tragedy. A moment's thrill is hardly worth a lifetime, or an eternity of pain or guilt.

Youthful affection is not always genuine, and is sometimes the product of confusion and insecurity. Youthful sex play is often impulsive—unrelated to a sincere, personal relationship. Too often, it is based on fears, a desire to be accepted, feelings of inadequacy, misinformation, immaturity or lack of self-control. Young people are well advised not to be intimidated by the "If I don't have a Saturday night date, I'm just no good" syndrome. They should rather associate socially in groups which respect and protect the rights of individuals who don't want to be pressured into compromising their standards, and by participating in constructive group activity. The young woman whose security and self-esteem is based on dates and the whim of young men is talking herself into a good deal of unnecessary unhappiness.

WHAT IS TRULY BEAUTIFUL?

In order to master the fire of sex rather than be consumed by it, Judaism teaches the virtue and value of *tsnius* or modesty. The idea of *tsnius* differs fundamentally from the non-Jewish concept of *chastity*, which bears the connotation of prudishness and ignorance, arising from an underlying Puritanic-Christian notion of the human body as evil and "flesh as sinful".

The Torah concept of *tsnius* bears connotations of restraint, privacy, good taste and dignity, which arise from the underlying acceptance of the human body as a vessel of man's sacred soul. The body should always be properly and tastefully covered, in order to preserve a sense of dignity, worth and self-respect, rather than openly flaunted and thus debased. To the Jew, *tsnius* is a major element of true beauty. True beauty lies not in what we reveal but in that which we conceal. Only a body properly clothed, not openly flaunted, is a fitting vessel for containing the true human beauty which lies beneath the surface of the physical self.

True feminine beauty has little in common with the artificial image of beauty projected by American cosmetic firms, television screens and advertising industries. The notion that true beauty, allure or happiness is determined by the extent to which a girl approaches the *ideal* in a physical sense is so much deceptive nonsense. The *ideal* is an arbitrary and often cruel standard that causes much needless unhappiness for those who take it too seriously, and as a result become slaves to a stereotyped notion of beauty. It is, in fact, an unmerciful hoax perpetrated by the false values of an over-commercialized, over-materialistic and sexually preoccupied society.

Real feminine beauty is a highly subjective, personal matter. It relates to the totality of the image and presence of an individual's personality. It is much more a reflection of poise, bearing, sensitivity, charm and values, than of any specific physical feature.

Young women, no matter how physically attractive, remain unconvinced inwardly of their own real beauty until they begin to love and be loved. Many obviously beautiful girls have sincerely protested, "But I'm not pretty". This suggests two possible insights: first, that true beauty exists "in the eyes of the beholder"—that beauty is largely a subjective highly personal phenomenon that gains true meaning in the context of marriage; second, that a truly beautiful person is one who loves and gives to another.

Both the conviction of beauty and mature love develop fully, deepen and are nurtured only in the context of married life. Many women feel "beautiful" only after they have been so convinced by the devotion, actions and attitudes of their loving husbands. This will explain why many girls who do not fit the stereotype, and are not beautiful by Madison Avenue criteria, are loved, admired and regarded as being highly attractive and desirable by their husbands. In simple terms, a woman's inner feeling of desirability and beauty may be an outgrowth and reflection of her husband's love. By the same token, a devoted wife is by far a more satisfying manifestation of a man's masculinity than any number of casual conquests of which he may be able to boast.

In a sustained marital relationship, the external physical criteria of sexual attractiveness are reduced to their rightful, secondary role, and the primary personality factors become dominant. In marriage, one soon discovers that deeds and attitudes are far more important than artificial standards of beauty. A wife's priorities and problems must become the husband's priorities and problems—and *vice versa*. There must be mutual dedication to common goals and to each other's well being. Lacking these ingredients, all the physical attractions in the world will not sustain a relationship, or provide long run happiness for either party.

When King Solomon said, "Charm is deceptive, and beauty is vain; but the woman who fears God is worthy of praise" (Proverbs 31:30), he meant, according to Rabbi Elijah the Ga'on of Vilna, that charm is deceitful and beauty false only when they are not accompanied by the fear of Heaven, for then they are nothing but external features. But if a beautiful and charming woman possesses the fear of Heaven, she is then worthy of praise. True beauty must radiate from within outward, and must relate to deeper qualities as well, not to external and painted-on beauty. Therefore, while Jewish tradition recognizes beauty as a factor in a woman's total personality, the woman who lacks values and reveals that which should remain concealed is considered not beautiful, but ugly and vulgar.

CLOTHES AND SHAME

The clothes we wear are closely related to the way we feel and act, the way a person dresses reveals a great deal about his personality and values. A person dressed immodestly feels freer to act less modestly, so that lack of restraint in dress may often be a first step toward lack of restraint in behavior and an indication of an inner lack of restraint.

The clothes we wear relate very closely to our sense of shame. When the eyes of Adam and Eve were "opened" and they became enlightened, their first awareness was of their naked state. The consciousness of being naked, rooted in the feeling of shame, and the awareness of the ability to choose, was the foundation of civilized society and the first step toward humanity. God has planted within us an inner feeling that restrains us from uncovering our nakedness, an unconscious guardian of our bodies that signals danger when we are about to falter.

This sense of shame can be destroyed, degraded or injured, just as we can pervert or suppress other natural inner feelings that God has planted within us. Shame protects our image of ourselves as moral people, and reinforces our sense of identification with the Torah people, which aspires to be a holy people.

Rabbi Dr. Joseph Breuer wrote that,

> Shame is something you feel as soon as you go astray and act contrary to the will of God. It calls out to you; 'What you just did was ugly, it was contemptible.' And it warns you never to do it again. Nurture this feeling within you, do not stifle it, and if you ever find that a friend of yours has lost that feeling of shame, then avoid his or her company.

A basic mark of the civilized man, which distinguishes him from the animals, is that he wears clothes. One major difference between *tsnius* (hiddenness) and its opposite *pritzus*, which means to reveal or break forth, by tearing down the walls and restraints of privacy and dignity, is in the way we relate to clothes. *Tsnius* uses clothes to conceal, thus creating sanctity, dignity and refinement, while *pritzus* uses clothes to reveal, thus degrading and dehumanizing our physical features. Our private features, in the Torah view, must be hidden from the eyes of others in order to maintain our dignity and self-respect, and to preserve each person for his or her chosen partner alone.

The first indication that we are in the presence of a vulgar and insensitive person is that the person has no hesitation to reveal his or her body. It makes little difference that the clothes have the blessing of "style" or the sanction of ten full-color pages in *Vogue* or the Sunday *New York Times Magazine*. To our society's discredit, its most popular fashions are all too often provocative and brazen. The woman who wears low cut, or revealing garments deliberately designed to display her body is shamelessly exposed. The *halachah*, fully aware of how easily the instinct for modest dress and modesty can be blunted by the daily assault of the mass media and the social environment, set forth specific dress standards for both men and women: Nearly every woman who is physically developed enough to have *what to reveal* instinctively knows just what parts of her body have erotic overtones and should therefore remain covered in order to keep safely within the bounds of propriety and *tsnius*. Because so many "styles" have of late gained acceptance, it is difficult, even for a fine young woman to avoid clothes that *halachah* would consider borderline. But there are usually sufficient choices and options to enable a person to be in style without being a slave to style. When a choice must be made between fashion and *tsnius*, a Jew must make that choice, sacrifices and difficulties notwithstanding. In today's society, where nudity in the movies and the media have become commonplace, and where non-modest dress has become the norm, it is often an act of true heroism and courage to dress modestly, as required by Jewish Law.

LOVE: INFATUATION AND ROMANCE, BUT MUCH MORE

Modern novels, movies, magazines, and television programs which fantasize and glorify the notion of "romantic love" are describing a type of ideal relationship that may exist in literary form or in the poetic imagination, but which bears very little resemblance to what love is all about in the everyday world of real life. People who read love stories or watch television programs should realize that while courtship, chivalry, romance, and passion do play their separate and respective roles in the dramatic awakening and eventual attainment of satisfaction in love, these are all elements in a process, but they do not by any means add up to the whole of the love experience. Nor is romantic love an end in itself, so that it cannot and should not be accepted in defense of any type of behavior in any male-female relationship which is less than a properly controlled one.

Such explanations as "We couldn't help ourselves, we just fell in love", or "we didn't realize what was happening" are excuses, not reasons, because people usually *do* realize very well indeed, what is happening; they all too often try to convince themselves that certain forms of intimacy are less reprehensible because the two individuals concerned happen to be *truly* in love. To fool oneself through this tactic is to lose control over oneself. Romantic love is not always related to real love, especially when it ignores the true personalities and mutual interest of those involved. To be ruled by one's emotions and feelings, uncontrolled and undirected by logic, values and clear thinking, with no clear sense of goals and responsibility, is to ignore the only factors which can establish a firm foundation for a permanent and mature lifelong relationship.

The theme repeated everywhere in novels and movies is that "I am in love and my love is beyond my control"; "I *fell* in love"; it was as though someone pushed me off a cliff and it was all accidental and unintentional. The Jewish approach warns us not to "love in spite of yourself", but to love "because of yourself". Find out what you're headed for. Enter into the love relationship with your eyes open, not with your eyes closed. Don't accept *blind* dates, unless you know who the potential partner is. If you find that you are "falling", realize while your eyes are still open, while you can still think clearly and objectively, who this person is for whom you are falling. By whom, I refer to background, commitment, education, character, personality, family, friends, values, concern for others, goals and ideals—the things that really count—not the external, superficial things, some of which may be "put on".

Fall in love with the real person inside the skin and not with a certain outward curvature of the flesh which may arouse your physical desire. Fall in love deliberately, with control, not on the rebound, or because you're simply "in love with love". Fall in love only after you have come to know yourself, not because you feel insecure and think "no one loves me", and not because you don't get along with your parents and are anxious to leave home. Don't let your craving for acceptance or love lead you to throw yourself at the first person who gives you a tumble or is "pliable" in sexual matters.

All this is a matter of decency, honesty and fairness to yourself, to the other person involved, and to your family and Jewish tradition. It is a precondition of authentic and lasting love. Let the woman use her "feminine charm"; it's her legitimate prerogative, a healthy manifestation of her femininity. It's quite one thing to be charmed by it, but don't be taken in; don't let it blind you; don't *fall* for it. If you take the romantic love angle too seriously, you will lose your proper place in the marital relationship and, with it, lose your dignity and your role as master of your destiny.

Young men, too, often employ a trickery more harmful and more dangerous than that employed by women. There is no ultimate danger if a girl employs her femininity to charm a young man into turning a fleeting interest into a more serious one. Young men, however, sometimes deceive a young woman into thinking that they are in love, while all they want is sex. Sex without true love, commitment and permanence is a price too high to pay.

CHOOSING A HUSBAND OR WIFE

In making the most crucial decision of his or her life, a young person often feels alone and abandoned. He or she needs someone who can be trusted, a person who has not only experience but also only the best interest of the other person at heart. Parents who think their children may not want or need help in deciding about marriage are often greatly mistaken. A parent who offers a well considered opinion, or who helps protect a son or daughter from being pressured into marriage by friends who often use subtle, or not so subtle means of pushing each other into marriage, can contribute a great deal toward the future happiness and success of the child's marriage.

Of course, no one would suggest that a parent make the ultimate decision, but children *do*, more often than one might expect, feel grateful for a parent's help in checking on the background of a possible partner or in evaluating his or her particular suitability in the given situation.

Many young people who date for the purpose of finding a mate do not want to become involved in going out with a person who does not meet their basic definition of a suitable husband or wife. It is obvious that the individual must make the ultimate decision. This decision will come about after meeting a few, or even many scores of young men or women. But *before* they go out, many young people appreciate if their parents discreetly investigate the young man or woman by whom they have been asked out, or in whom they are interested, to determine whether they should be taken into consideration. Sons and daughters often have a whole list of required, and another list of preferred qualifications. The task of parents is to see to it that dating is not left to chance, that it is not an accidental process. They and their son or daughter are entitled to know beforehand the qualities and qualifications of the young man or woman. Many young people I have spoken to refuse to go out unless their parents have inquired first about the other's plans, character, aspirations, background, ideals, goals, education, personality, accomplishments, etc. "Why waste time", they say, "or take chances with someone who does not *begin* to come into consideration".

In an article entitled "Good Marriages, The Failure of Success", Dr. Reuven P. Bulka compares the differences in approach to marriage between Eastern and Western civilization (*RCA Newsletter*, 1978). He writes:

> One of the problems with Western civilization is that people tend to think only in logical terms. This precludes the potent impact of the mystical dimension in human behavior. As an example, Ernest Havermann once pointed out that in the East, people get married and then they fall in love, whilst in the West they fall in love and then get married.
>
> The logician, according to Havermann, would think that the Western way is more reasonable and that one must take things in their proper order. However, Havermann points out, contrary to the logician's projection, the Eastern way actually works better.
>
> In fact, by approaching marriage along logical lines, Western civilization has robbed marriage of its most vital ingredient, the element of "shared destiny". Marriage is approached too often in the West along the lines of a mathematical equation. If the times spent together add up to satisfaction, then the couple assumes that future times together will bring more satisfaction; and on this basis the marriage union is finally consummated. Where the process is reversed, however, and one obviously chooses a mate based on common background, values shared, and a somewhat common view of life, marriage becomes a

shared destiny, where the sharing of common values and a simultaneous affirmation of past, present, and future link the couple together in deep understanding, which ultimately brings the side benefit of real love. This is the process described in the Torah, in Genesis 24: 67, where it is related that "Isaac took Rebecca as his wife and he loved her", indicating the Eastern sequence, that is, first they married, and then came love.

The major point, of course, is that rather than seeing marriage as an end in itself, Judaism sees it as a vehicle which helps human beings attain the higher values of life. The focus of the Jewish marriage is not on the marriage, but on the values and goals of husband and wife individually, and in their lives together. The sum total of their relationship adds up to Jewish destiny. This explains why in so many Jewish marriages the needs and education of children are often placed before the satisfactions of the married couple. In a true marriage, destiny and values are placed *before* pleasure and personal needs.

It is a matter of urgency that marriage be restored as a commitment that transcends the individual partners. Marriage attaches males to families, and this is the source of human continuity, individuality, and growth. The family is the one institution of mankind that can bring about the greatest and most profound influences on its members. The family must again become *the* place to develop human character and a commitment to idealism and spirituality.

We often think of the Torah primarily as a book of laws, while in truth the Torah places its *greatest* emphasis on the life stories of people. The entire book of Genesis is devoted to describing the lives and families of Abraham, Isaac, Jacob and Joseph. The reason for this emphasis on people is that the Torah wants us to relate to our ancestors not as remote historical personages, but as parents and grandparents. The fathers are more than the founders of the Jewish nation; the *fathers* are just that—*fathers*—founders of the families of Abraham, Isaac and Jacob. It is the aim of the Torah that we learn from their example, emulate them, and see them as role models after whom to pattern our lives. Most of all, the Torah expects us to see ourselves as members of their immediate family, so that we will continue to live their dreams and fulfill their aspirations.

CASUAL AND MORE SERIOUS PURPOSES OF DATING

It is the general American attitude that boys and girls date for fun, for pleasure, or for simple entertainment. But if the purpose of an evening out is so *completely* casual, then why don't boys simply go to the movies with boys and girls with girls?

The answer is obvious. There is a completely normal, healthy, and quite universally operative attraction between the sexes that begins pulling boys and girls together during adolescence, and which leads to the process of courtship and eventually to the conclusion of marriage. So dating isn't the *completely* casual or platonic affair one might try to convince oneself it is. There is usually some type of physical or chemical attraction involved.

The above accepted, one must realize that dating in general is always part of the search-for-husband-or-wife process. One's road to the marriage canopy may be long or short. One may meet the right person on the first date, after only a few dates, or may not meet the right person for years, so great care must, for safety's sake, be exercised in all choices one makes. A framework for restraint in behavior must be clearly defined and understood between one and each one of the people one chooses to date along the way.

While the immediate goal of a date may be for the simple fun of an evening out, the underlying purposes or ultimate results of dating are the purposes of serious courtship and eventual marriage. For this reason, the entire dating process should be considered very seriously and very deliberately. A person should take care *never* even casually to date another person he or she knows from the start he or she could never marry.

Every meeting with the opposite sex is related, in some way, to mating, to the mysterious force that calls two people to join as one in marriage. So it should be. It is very rare to find a genuine platonic relationship or "just friendship" between the sexes. The normal sexual attraction, the pull of the opposites, is always at work.

A person doesn't dare get into an old car to enjoy a drive without first checking whether or not the brakes are in proper working order. You may say to yourself, "I am not going for a ride with any particular destination in mind, just for a little ride around the corner. My intention is not serious, it's just for fun". If, however, when you reach the first corner, you apply the brakes and they fail, your joy ride could change the course of your life. In much the same way, a "casual date" could be just as fateful.

THE DANGERS OF INTERMARRIAGE

There may be a beautiful gentile girl living a few houses away from you. You may never in all your life dream of marrying her, and your relationship has probably not gone further than a polite "Hello", as you pass each other on the street. Then one day you decide to take her out, *just for the fun of it*, maybe to *show her off*, to *show them* that you can be seen with such a beautiful girl. Your intention is just for fun—one evening out and that's it. (This example applies just as well in the case of a gentile boy dating a Jewish girl.)

That may be *your* intention, but keep in mind that it may not be hers. During the first date, she may decide that you are exactly what she wants. The fact is, that in making the first approach, you have left yourself open to an honest assumption on her part; "If I'm good enough to go out with, I'm good enough to marry". Women have their ways and their charms, and if they put their minds to getting something, you may in the end succumb. The fellow who is foolish enough to get himself into this kind of difficulty is rarely smart enough to get himself out of it. By putting a young man and woman, two *inflammable* objects together, it is only natural to anticipate the possibility of an emotional explosion. To ignore the possibility is to practice self-deception.

The conclusion is obvious. Whenever one goes out, it is possible, despite the fact that one's intellectual defenses are up, that one's emotional defenses are down. The very nature of the dating experience sets up conditions for the formation of permanent relationships.

One criterion for maturity is the ability to give up present pleasure for future gain. It is the child who wants all pleasures immediately, without regard for consequences. To be an adult means to have acquired the ability to resist temptation; to say *no*; to live by a set of values.

Intermarriage is a tragedy the Jewish people cannot tolerate. The person who marries out of the faith has turned his or her back on the Jewish people. Our tradition regards such a person as spiritually dead, and the family sits *shiva* for him or her.

Such marriages rarely work, even when accompanied by a so-called conversion to Judaism, and certainly can never work when the Jewish partner is seriously concerned with his or her Jewishness. For the families involved, the result is heartbreak and tragedy, and for the children, a life of frustration, conflict and strain.

6
Tsnius:
An Essential Element
for Holiness

THE BEHAVIOR OF JEWISH WOMEN

Through her behavior, dress and talk, a young woman has an effect upon a young man which she is sometimes unable to appreciate and evaluate. By conducting herself in a refined, reserved fashion, as commanded by the Torah, a young woman preserves her own dignity and self-respect, and does not compromise herself or the qualities which should make her a fine wife and mother. If she carelessly flaunts and displays her physical self, she arouses feelings in the opposite sex which may, in the long run, prove to be her undoing. Some women degrade themselves by using their appearance, charm and favors as currency to bargain for "desirable dates". This often gives them a false status of popularity, which is even harder to maintain without further compromise.

A Jew must always be careful to refrain from any kind of public conduct or appearance that could arouse erotic desire in a person of the opposite sex. Nothing in man–woman relationships remains *innocent* for long. It is rare that a physically mature young woman will fail to stimulate a young man, unless she is careful to act in a restrained fashion. My intention is not to vindicate the man for improper behavior or to place blame on the woman; still there are some basic differences.

It is interesting to note that this observation is not unique to the Torah point of view. In a *Reader's Digest* article by Sugarman and Hochstein, the difference between the reactions of young men and women to sexual stimuli was spelled out in the following terms:

There is a great biological and emotional difference between adolescent boys and girls. Sexual desire comes to boys in a great rush of emotion—an immediate, specific desire, quite apart from the deeper emotions of love and tenderness. While some girls separate love from physical attraction, most find their sexual desires closely bound to feelings of romantic love. Unlike a boy's, a girl's sexual drives and her heart figuratively work together. Boys, then, are likely to be much more casual about sex than are girls—but they are also more urgent in the immediate moment of sexual encounter. Unless a girl understands this psychology, she is bound to be confused when a boy makes advances to her. It doesn't mean that he loves her.

So it isn't an insult if a boy 'makes a pass' at you; in a sense, that's his nature. But it is also not an insult to him when you refuse. Your own slower-rising, longer lasting emotions are your protection against the consequences of allowing a boy's urgency to prevail—consequences which are much more serious to a girl than to a boy.

While this analysis does not describe the behavior of Jewishly committed young women, it does contain insights which should serve as a warning for them to become more conscious of the way their dress, behavior and talk can affect the young men around them. While to some young men this kind of conduct may, unfortunately, be part of "the game", to a young woman her conduct is, and always should be, "serious business". All too often, a young woman becomes involved in serious difficulties because she somehow has "asked for it" by repeatedly behaving in a manner not befitting her status as a daughter of Israel.

None of the above is an excuse for male excess or lack of restraint. *Anyone* who violates the laws of society or Torah is considered culpable and held responsible to pay the penalty of his or her action. The whole point of the Torah is to help men and women accustom themselves to a life of discipline and self-restraint.

Tsnius, it should be pointed out, relates not only to behavior and dress, but to language and conversation as well.

Our Sages (Talmud *Shabbos* 33) tell us, "Everyone knows why the bride enters the bridal chamber". Yet they condemn violently anyone who speaks of this relationship in vulgar terms. Why? The introductory phrase of the Talmudic passage explains: "Everyone knows why".

For the Torah Jew, romance and the sexual relationship are neither vulgar nor sinful—but talking about them in vulgar or crude terms has no place in the conduct of religious men or women.

The very meaning of the word "*tsnius*", variously translated as privacy, hiddenness, or modesty, points to an attitude which abhors the modern passion for exposing to public view the hiddenness and privacy of an intensely personal relationship. And if this attitude relates to the actual relationship, it relates even more so to talking about it openly in company.

If the author has been careful to point out that young men are no less responsible than young women for behaving modestly, temperately, and reservedly in male-female relationships, however casual or intensely personal, then why is the term *tsnius*, with all it implies, usually associated with female conduct and almost never with male? Why are women held so much more responsible than men in this realm of *tsnius*—modesty in dress and behavior?

A number of explanations might be advanced. First, a woman has much more at stake. For her, the consequences of rash, impulsive, or thoughtless behavior can change the course of her entire life overnight. While a man can easily get up and walk away from a casual affair, with the door closed behind him, a woman may carry the result of that casual affair as a physical, social, or psychological burden for the remainder of her entire life.

A second idea comes from the Midrash, *Breishis Raba* 18:2, which suggests that a special aspect of woman's nature is the capacity to take one facet of human personality and develop it to its highest expression. This trait, the Midrash suggests, is the capacity for *tsnius*.

Rabbi Moshe Meiselman, in his article on "Women and Judaism" (*Tradition*, Fall 1975), offers a third set of explanations. He says:

> The root *tzena* is mentioned twice in the Bible, once as we have already seen in the verse, 'That he who toils in the wisdom of Torah in private, will achieve wisdom.' (Proverbs 11:2) And secondly in the verse in Micha: 'He has told you man what is good and what the Lord demands from you, nothing else but to do justice, to love kindness and to walk privately with your God.' (Micha 6:8) When one serves God, he must concentrate on the inner dimensions of his personality. *Tsnius* is the inner dimension of one's striving, which is the essence of the Jewish

heroic act. It is this trait of personality that woman was enjoined to develop to its highest degree. Thus woman was created from a part of the body which is private in two senses—first that it is generally clothed and second that it is located beneath the skin.

But, hidden from public view, does not imply inferiority. It is thus in Genesis that when the angels visited Abraham and asked him, where is Sarah your wife, Abraham answered, "In the tent" (Genesis 18:9) to which *Rashi* cites the comment of the Rabbis, "Sarah was a private person". Yet, on a spiritual level, we find that Sarah achieved greater stature than Abraham, "All that Sarah tells you, hearken to her voice", (Genesis 21:12) to which Rashi comments, "This teaches us that Sarah was superior to Abraham in prophecy". Although in their life together, Abraham took the public role, this implied absolutely nothing about personal importance or spiritual greatness. For the Jewish hero is the hero of the inner stage, not one of the public stage.

A WOMAN SETS THE TONE

There are certain roles that have been filled traditionally by women within the framework and structure of Jewish life, in order for certain important interests to be served and for Jewish tradition to retain its vitality and strength from one generation to the next. If, however, in the process of fulfilling her obligations to husband, family, and Jewish life, a woman feels that she has time, energy, and emotional strength enough to pursue additional interests as well, or if she finds that a certain amount of time devoted to the pursuit of other interests will enable her to serve better in the capacities of wife and mother, the Torah would certainly never restrict her freedom to make such judgments, as long as the priorities of responsibility are never confused and as long as she does not, in the process, compromise her effectiveness in the scheme of Jewish life.

To be a successful woman, according to the Torah view, can constitute one of life's greatest, most difficult, yet most noble challenges.

It is the woman who binds husband and children to herself in that magical relationship of love, devotion, and loyalty that all together generate the warmth and security of family life. To give unselfishly of her love, and be the recipient of so much love, must surely constitute a source of great fulfillment in a woman's life. Woman is the cement which holds together the family and all of society. To woman alone did God entrust the supreme role of motherhood, so important and primary a task that the Torah exempted women from most of the time-bound positive commandments, such as *t'fillin*, *tsitsit*, or *sukkah*. A woman's tasks are timeless—that is, above and beyond time—and are considered too important in the scheme of things to be pre-empted by any other day-to-day schedule of conflicting obligations. The woman's greatest, overriding positive responsibility is to household, children, and husband. Her home is the great school, sanctuary, and laboratory of Jewish life. And the task of directing this institution, where a positive, Torah saturated environment is created and maintained, rests primarily on the woman's shoulders. The raising of children demands constant attention. A woman cannot possibly be tied down to other responsibilities of the sort that would interfere with her effectiveness at home unless some other person, equally as effective and reliable, is put in charge. A woman's primary area of responsibility within the context of Jewish life then rests in the management of family and home; nothing may interfere with the proper execution of these vital tasks.

The work of a mother in the job of raising children and molding personalities might be compared to the work of a great architect at the table with his blueprints, or to the work of a scientist in the laboratory with his instruments. They are all trying, with the most effective blend possible of skill, art, instinct, ingenuity, knowledge, and intelligent application, to achieve the end of a useful, successful, and worthwhile product or creation.

But even the work of the scientist or architect is insignificant and uncreative when compared to a mother at her job of molding a personality—the personality of a child. In doing so she is molding and recreating all humanity.

WOMAN'S NATURE IS UNIQUE

Another reason for woman's exemption from time-bound positive commandments is that she does not require them in order to achieve fulfillment as a full person. To quote from Dr. Norman Lamm in his *Hedge of Roses* (page 75):

> She is already aware of the sanctification of time in a manner far more profound, far more intimate and personal, and far more

convincing than that which a man can attain by means of the extraneous observances which he is commanded. For woman, unlike man, has a built-in biological clock. The periodicity of her menses implies an inner biological rhythm that forms part and parcel of her life. If this inner rhythm is not sanctified, she never attains the sanctity of time.

The man attains this sense of sanctity of time only through the time-bound positive commandments associated with the time of day, week and month, from which woman is exempt.

A woman is already involved every day, and almost all of her time is bound up in the observance of other kinds of Torah commandments, so that her life is far more saturated with religious activity than the average man's life could possibly be, and her opportunity for spiritual development is almost unlimited. For instance, in the management of her household, she is involved with the observance of Kashruth law; in the rearing of her children with the observances of Limud and Talmud Torah law; in the relationship with her husband with the observance of Family Purity law; and in preparing herself, her household, and all members of her family for Shabbat and Festivals, with the observance of Shabbat and Festival law. A man, however, can only attain the same sense of sanctity in his life through involvement with other sorts of commandments, more associated with the time of day, week, month, or year, and hence called time-bound, from which woman is exempt.

ATTACK ON THE FAMILY

The most dangerous and fatal manifestation of the new morality comes when it denigrates the role of family or the importance of commitment to the idea of family. The fact that half of all American marriages end in divorce is evidence enough to indicate the instability and weakness of that commitment in the attitudes of present day Americans.

Any attack on the family is no less dangerous than genocide, in that it is a blow struck at the very basis of all well-ordered and smoothly functioning society. Because the family is the source and center of human love, kindness, intimacy, and companionship, it is no accident that it is the pivot of all society and that Jewish society is therefore considered a collective of families, not of individuals. Rav Chama Bar Chanina of the Talmud (Kiddushin 10) said that "When God causes His *Sh'china* (or Divine Presence) to dwell in the Jewish People, He does so by causing it to dwell in the midst of the worthy families (*mishpochos meyuchosos*) of Israel".

The woman, therefore, who is the foundation of the family, is particularly responsible to consider the preservation of its core, strength, and integrity, She is called *akeres habayis*, or foundation and mainstay of the home. In shaping the personality and in setting the tone, standards, and values of the home, by extension she guides the development of all society. And although her day-to-day accomplishments may often be measured in terms of her husband's success or her children's achievements, in a broader sense she is responsible, as a result of her determined efforts, for the success of all human endeavor. No wonder that God said to Abraham (Genesis 21:12), "Do not fail to do just as your wife Sarah instructs you, because it is through her son, Issac, that you will have the descendants I have promised".

The above attitude is not a patronizing rationalization invoked to satisfy a society challenged by the heightened consciousness of thinking women. Wherever Jews have achieved greatness, whenever they have shown spiritual progress or regeneration, there have been women at the center: idealistic, selfless, highly motivated, and willing to sacrifice. It was the wives who were prepared to raise their families, sometimes with only the bare necessities, so that their husbands could devote themselves to Torah scholarship.

The revival of Torah scholarship in America, for instance, has been largely due to the idealism and commitment of women who have either worked hard to translate an inspired concept into reality through day schools for their children or who have encouraged their husbands to devote themselves to Torah scholarship.

The wives of successful men are seldom passive and self-effacing. To the contrary, they are usually forceful, insistent, influential, and directive.

THE WORK OF A WOMAN AS MOTHER

In bearing and raising children, the woman participates in the most creative and unique miracle on God's earth. She has given birth and is in charge of the creation and formation of human beings—the unique creation of her love, devotion, her very body, for which her skills, instincts and temperament are specially designed.

Are the chores of mother and housewife beneath a woman's dignity? When a woman is cooking or cleaning, sewing for or bathing her children, is she reducing herself to a lowly or servile level? Or is the time she spends teaching her children to be honest, fair, sensitive, and self-confident wasted or spent needlessly? Why should it seem more prestigious to "fire" a clay pot than to "bake" an apple pie? Why should it be considered more creative to cook for a restaurant than for a family? Or again, why should a woman gain greater status by working as a child psychologist, in the counselling of other people's children, than she would by staying home to supervise her own? Or finally, is there any good reason why the woman who holds a formal teaching position teaching other people's children, should be more highly regarded than the woman who stays home to teach her own children?

If it *is* only paid performance that society respects, then what shall be the future of such terms as were used formerly to characterize the more meaningful activities of men and women for which they were *not paid*, such as "love", "kindness", "generosity", "nobility", "dedication", or the like? Shall these terms, with all they convey, be simply striken from the dictionary and from the thinking and behavioral habits of men?

That the Hebrew word for "womb" (*rechem*) and the Hebrew word for "mercy" (*rachamim*) derive from the same root indicates that in the very roots of its language, Jewish tradition considered the attributes of mercy and compassion as both natural and essential to the function of a woman in carrying, in giving birth to, and in rearing her children. If a woman will not set an example, where will her husband or children learn the attitudes of caring, and where, if not from the lesson of the family, will the human community at large learn the lessons of accountability, responsibility, and regard, every man, woman and child for his or her neighbor?

THE ROLE OF THE WIFE IN CREATING MAN

The role of the wife in maintaining the centrality of the family relates not only to the raising of children, but to the creating of the context of family and home so that men too can function effectively in society. As our sages have said, "A man's wife is his home". If the wife does not feel her role keenly and deeply, then the husband will find great difficulty in forming his own deep relationship to the family. It is the wife who cements the family through physical and emotional ties created by her personality, her attractiveness, and her ability to integrate her husband into the family by promoting and deepening the shared relationships of love and responsibility—which express themselves in the creation of children.

Essentially, the family is the mother's kingdom. The father must create and mold his function and role within the family by becoming a responsible breadwinner, and by becoming involved in the decision making process, while the role of mother is more natural.

In general, woman's role and self-definition are much more obvious than man's. Man must *make* something of himself to *become* a man. Without study, accomplishment and skills—without proving himself—he forever remains a child. A man must constantly demonstrate and prove his role, to himself, to his parents and to his wife, before he believes in himself as a man. From the very beginning, a boy's self-identity as a male is dependent upon acts of creativity and initiative.

In a biological sense, woman is *born* woman. She is created whole and complete, while man is born incomplete. A man must be circumcised in order to *become* a man; something must be *done* to him to make him a man. The act of circumcision, I believe, sets the pattern which follows all through a man's life. He must constantly "*circumcise*" himself, prove himself and make something of himself. Man must always be outwardly creative in order to become and remain himself.

The above can be demonstrated by observing the physical development of man and woman. Outwardly, a boy appears essentially the same even as he passes from boyhood to adolescence to maturity. Compared to the changes that take place in a maturing woman, the physical changes in the man are minor as he matures into manhood. Outwardly, physically, a man's appearance is essentially the same at six, at ten, at fourteen and at eighteen. A girl, however, may *look* much like a boy before adolescence, but when she matures, the internal and external transformation is so striking and so significant that it is quite evident that she has *become* a woman.

Woman's personality is a reflection of her biology. In this sense a woman is much more *woman* than a man is *man*. A woman *need* not be creative in an external sense in order to become a woman. No matter what else she may do outside of the home, no matter what areas of creativity she may be involved in, her highest creation is internal—within herself. A woman does not need to be circumcised because she is born complete, her femininity dominates her being, appearance and personality. The only external event that causes a fundamental change in a woman is her relationship with a man. Only then does something external enter her body, and transform her into a wife and mother.

Woman's self-identity is clear and stable. Her role as a wife and mother is a manifestation of her biology and appearance. Her internal and external biology define and describe her. In addition, the woman's gender is demonstrated and affirmed monthly by menstruation. Even if she does not bear a child, she is constantly reminded that she *can*—that only *she* can perpetuate her family and mankind. No matter what anxieties or crises society is undergoing with regard to defining the role of men and women, the woman *knows* that she has a role. This knowledge is stamped on her very being.

While the female body is full of intricately constructed internal and external structures and potential for creativity—womb, breasts, etc.—the male is essentially barren. To be expressed, defined and achieved, manhood demands action. Man, therefore, is deeply dependent upon the *structure* of society in order to find himself.

Of all of the structures of society, marriage is the most basic and important. Not only for all the reasons spelled out above—but also because marriage attaches men to families. Thus, families are society's source of continuity and creativity.

The family is the one social structure that can most effectively bring about changes in the character and commitment of society. But most important, the family is the only instrument which turns men into voluntary participants in the development of a healthy society.

Why did God prefer Isaac's son, Jacob, to Esau? Esau is described by the Torah as a "man of the field". Rabbi Samson Raphael Hirsch says that Esau believed that the essence of human creativity takes place in the "field", in the "market place" of man's world, in the great world of commerce and industry. But Jacob was the "complete man who lived in the tent". He centered his life around the "tent", the home. To Jacob, the family and the home were *the* focal point of life. "Jacob recognized and taught that the highest mission of life lies in achieving the knowledge and practice to be obtained in the sphere of the homes of mankind". It is for this reason that he merited to receive his father's blessing and to become the father of the twelve tribes of Israel.

THE EQUALITY OF WOMEN

Is the Jewish woman man's equal? Our answer is a resounding yes, as long as we understand what is meant by that statement. Equality in value does not imply equality in function. Man and woman do not have the same function in life. The fact is that, in *her* areas of specialty, in her special realms, woman is far superior. Most of the earlier fighters for woman's equality falsely equated equality with forcing woman into man's mold (remember the men's clothes they once wore?). They wished women to be masculine and envisioned them as imitating man, and living in man's world on equal terms with men. It is our hope that in spite of the propaganda of women's liberation, Jewish women will continue to view the unique tasks of motherhood and family as *the* most rewarding, and will choose these roles above others. Even among women who pursue a "career" in addition to their families, most continue to insist that they are happiest and most productive when they can function as women and live in a "woman's world", not when they seek to emulate and imitate the man's role. The differences between the sexes are far more than physical. They relate to woman's special nature, talents, mentality and temperament which are so different from man's. Woman is psychologically and emotionally different in a thousand and one ways which range from sex, appearance and clothes to sensitivity, submissiveness and intuition.

The place where woman generally achieves the most and derives her most meaningful fulfillment is in her home. Here she is queen, and her rank of nobility must always be protected. While many Jewish women find constructive tasks outside of the home, serving as students, educators, youth leaders, social workers, nurses, physicians, business people, and in many other valuable occupations, these tasks are valid and rewarding only when the family and home are her "home base", and have first claim on her love, interest and loyalty, while the career or job is supplementary.

My wife always insists that she is a "working woman", not a "career woman". More than anything else, we are talking about priorities. What is the woman's source of personal identification, satisfaction and achievement? What takes priority when there are conflicts, the home or the job? A woman's career is her family; her job or profession are positive when they function as additional programs, secondary in importance to home and family. Jewish women have, throughout the ages, been especially prominent in private and communal efforts on behalf of the sick, the poor, the wayfarer, the new bride and the student. Philanthropy and help of those in need, *tsedakah* and *chesed*, are the special areas in which the Jewish woman excels. And when Jewish women entered the business world or pursued careers, as often has been the case in Jewish history throughout the world, it has invariably been to aid the common goals of her husband and children in pursuit of a life of *mitzvos* and Torah study.

THE SURPRISING BIBLICAL RECORD

It is paradoxical that the Jews and their Bible are often blamed for the negative attitudes towards women which exist in our society. This blame should rightfully be placed squarely on the doorsteps of the Greeks, the Romans and the pagans from whom Western civilization and Christianity drew those attitudes which led to present dissatisfactions.

Let's look at the Bible. 98% of the first book of the Bible, Genesis, is devoted to narratives describing the creation of the world, the beginnings of mankind, and the lives of Abraham, Isaac, Jacob and the Tribes of Israel. The reason Genesis dwells on biography, personalities, events and not laws is to instruct us to pattern our own lives on their struggles, their challenges and the solutions which they employed. Of course, were the Bible to have recorded the full biographies of Abraham, Isaac, Jacob and their children, many heavy volumes would have been required. Instead, the Bible selects very few incidents, because these specific events represent the special life situations which the Bible expects us to emulate.

Let's study a few examples relating to the "place" of women: Abraham and Sarah are childless. Sarah devises a plan to bear children by giving her handmaid to Abraham. She says, if my handmaid gives birth I will "be built up through her". The handmaid gives birth to a child, Ishmael. As Ishmael matures, Sarah comes to the painful conclusion that he will have a negative influence on her son, Isaac. As a result, she urges Abraham, "Banish your son, your first born son and his mother from this house". The Torah tells us that this request was "evil in the eyes of Abraham". Nonetheless, God comes to Abraham and tells him "Sarah is right and you are wrong". Do whatever Sarah tells you—because "it is only through Isaac that you will see posterity". The Rabbis teach that Sarah was "superior in prophecy to Abraham". Otherwise, why would God demand that Abraham follow Sarah's instructions? Abraham obeys God, banishes Ishmael and accedes to Sarah's demand. Thus begins the saga of the Jewish people.

In the next generation we read a similar story. Isaac, now a father, wants to give his blessing to his eldest son, Esau, and not to Jacob. Rebecca, the mother, disagrees. After failing to convince Isaac that she is right, she devises an elaborate plan of deception. She dresses Jacob in Esau's clothes and instructs him to impersonate Esau and take his blessing. Neither Rebecca nor Jacob are criticized for this deception. On the contrary, Jacob receives his father's blessing and becomes the founder of the Jewish people.

The important conclusion to be derived from this incident is that Rebecca acted on her own judgement, took the situation into her own hands—deceived her husband in order to preserve the Jewish people. It was her courage, her judgement, her wisdom and her action which created the Jewish people.

Later, the Jewish people are enslaved and oppressed in Egypt. The Talmud tells us that Amram, father of Moses, was the leader of that generation. When the Egyptians decreed that all male children be drowned, Amram decided that he could no longer bring children into the world. Therefore, he separated from his wife and all the Jewish men followed his lead. At that point his daughter, Miriam, demanded, "Father, your decree is more cruel than Pharaoh's. Pharaoh's decree applies to the male children alone. But yours applies to all children equally. Pharaoh's decree may or may not persist—but because you are a righteous man, your decree will persist". Miriam's insight convinces her father, he takes back his wife, and so do the others. As a result, Moses is born and thus begins the chain of events which result in the liberation and birth of the Jewish people.

In the desert, the Jews worship a golden calf. The Talmud relates that only the men were involved in this crime while the women refused to participate. When Aaron the High Priest solicited gold to construct the golden calf, the Torah informs us that the wives refused to part with their jewelry. The women, however, didn't simply refuse to surrender their jewelry because of a love for jewelry—because later on when the time came to build the Holy Tabernacle, we are told that the women were very generous in their contributions of gold.

Later on, while the Jewish people were still wandering in the desert, they decided to send spies to the Land of Israel prior to attempting to invade it. Ten spies returned with a frightening and negative report. "There is no way we can conquer the land", they reported. "Giants live there—the cities are walled to the heavens—their armies are much too powerful".

As a result, the Jews rebelled: "Why did you bring us out of Egypt to be slaughtered by our enemies?" they cried. As punishment, the Jews were forced to remain in the Sinai desert for an additional 38 years. Rashi, the most famous Biblical commentator, teaches that only the men rebelled—the women were prepared for whatever sacrifices were required in order to conquer the Land of Israel. Since the men rebelled, only they died in the desert while the women merited to enter the Land of Israel.

The bottom line in all of these incidents is that when faced with crisis, not only did the men and the women differ in their judgement, but the judgement of the women proved to be consistently correct while the men were wrong. In each and every instance, the women exercised independent judgement and freely disagreed with their husbands. Not only did the women possess independence of judgement, they possessed independence of action as well. Rebecca did not simply say, "I disagree". She acted on her convictions as well.

This is a far cry from the stereotyped "traditional Jewish women" we read about in so many articles and books.

Summary

JEWISH MODESTY IS NOT PRUDISHNESS

Jewish modesty is not prudishness or the fear of sex. The Torah speaks openly and frankly about sexual relations and the human body. The Biblical book "The Song of Songs", regarded by Rabbi Akiva as "holy of holies", even uses the imagery of physical love where "caresses are better than wine" to highlight the courtship of God and the Jewish people. This sacred book is replete with sensual Hebrew terms equivalent to such English words as "delight", "love", "beauty", "arouse", "beloved", "pleasant", "lovesick", "sweet", and "comely". So much is the Jew at home with the normal functioning of the human body that the very concept of "dirty word" is unknown in the Hebrew language. Hebrew is possibly the only language that doesn't have two sets of words to depict the body and its biological and sexual functions. The body and its functions were created by God and are sanctified through the love, confidence and mutual esteem of the family that observes the Torah principles of the "sanctity of the family".

The Torah is concerned with human dignity and with preserving the rights of our fellow man. In man himself, in his very body, resides the Divine spark breathed into him by his Creator. This body is not a toy designed merely for pleasure, but an instrument for molding and creating a world on God's pattern.

The laws and customs of *tsnius*, or modesty, are designed to help, not hinder Jewish men and women in the fulfillment of their own sexual and emotional needs. The laws of *tsnius* are designed to engender respect for, not fear of, sex. They are designed to encourage a healthy sense of taste, decency, and propriety in sexual behavior and do not seek to encourage repressive, prudish, or guilt-ridden attitudes. They attempt to define what is fitting, suitable, and appropriate to given times, places, and circumstances. Founded in the firm belief that there is much more to a bond of love than the simple idea of erotic or sensual pleasure, they distinguish between what is holy or vulgar, sacred or profane, noble or base, honorable or corrupt, refined or crude, civilized or barbarous, dignified or demeaned.

Sex is a private, personal matter. It relates to the most intimate bonds we can possibly establish with another person. It is a primary natural force which, together with other personality factors, comprises the cement which transforms two strangers into intimate, loving, life-long companions, committed to each other and to the building of a Jewish family. The laws of *tsnius* make possible a constructive and harmonious life by creating an atmosphere of restraint and dignity. Sex is not a public cult of the body. The repulsive emphasis on eroticism in modern American society is deliberately vulgar and cynically exploitative. The Torah by no means opposes sex, but it does condemn the *cult of sex*, and the false worship of it. The abuse and misuse of sex by immature and irresponsible people can turn this instrument for man's good into an instrument turned against man, used for the most evil and destructive ends.

The greater the potential of something for good, the worse it is when it is used for evil. Bad wine is far worse than bad water. The disintegrated corpse of a human being is far more obnoxious than the dead petals of a withered rose. Sex, when it is linked to love, and is used in accordance with the tested guidelines set forth by the Torah, can be the greatest and most beautiful life-giving force. When perverted and misused, it becomes an instrument for human misery. The Torah puts the responsibility squarely in our hands, "See, I have given you this day life and death, the good and the bad. Choose life".

J·E·W·I·S·H
ALTERNATIVES
IN
LOVE, DATING & MARRIAGE